HANDBOOK

OF

FIREWORK AND SIGNALLING STORES

IN USE BY

LAND, NAVAL, AND AIR SERVICES.

(BOMBS, CANDLES, CARTRIDGES, FLARES, GRENADES, LIGHTS, ROCKETS, SIGNALS, &c.)

1920.

The Naval & Military Press Ltd

Published by

The Naval & Military Press Ltd
Unit 5 Riverside, Brambleside
Bellbrook Industrial Estate
Uckfield, East Sussex
TN22 1QQ England

Tel: +44 (0)1825 749494

www.naval-military-press.com
www.nmarchive.com

In reprinting in facsimile from the original, any imperfections are inevitably reproduced and the quality may fall short of modern type and cartographic standards.

BOMBS.

BOMBS, 3·45-INCH, SIGNAL, FLARE, RED.

The **Mark I bomb** (Plate I) consists of a cylindrical rolled paper body with a coned head provided with a wood cap and closed at the bottom by a millboard disc glued in. A cupro-nickel electric contact strip is shellaced to opposite sides of the body, and a wooden guide to fit the launching tube is secured at right angles to the strips. Two wire leads from an electric tube are passed through saw-cuts made in the slope of the head, and soldered to the upper ends of the contact strips on the body.

The interior of the body is filled with red flare composition.

The body is coated with aluminium paint, a red band is painted round the centre to denote colour of flare, and a label giving the designation of the bomb is gummed on the side.

The **Mark II bomb** (Plate II) differs from the Mark I described above in having a hollow composite cap instead of a wood cap fitted in the head, and a length of Bickford fuze, No. 11 B, on top of which is placed a wad of priming composition, is secured down the centre instead of priming only as in the Mark I. There is also a slight difference in the arrangement of the quickmatch, which is looped on to the Bickford fuze.

BOMB, 3·45-INCH, SIGNAL, FLARE, WHITE, MARK I.

This **bomb** (Plate III) consists of a tin cylinder lined with rolled paper closed at the top with a wood head as described for the red flare bomb, Mark I, and also having similar contact strips and electric firing arrangement. The bottom is closed with a wood block and a millboard disc. The bomb is filled with aluminium composition, and the exterior is painted with aluminium paint with a red filling ring stencilled near the head.

BOMB, 3·45-INCH, SIGNAL, SMOKE.

The **Mark I bomb** (Plate IV) consists of a tin cylinder covered with rolled paper closed at the top with a wood head as described for the red flare bomb, Mark I (above), also having similar contact strips and firing arrangement. It contains smoke composition in the upper portion of the body and a black cashmere parachute in the lower portion, which is closed by a tin cup.

(B 15081) Wt. w. 103—PP3656 1м 9/20 H & S Ltd. Misc. 82.

Bombs, 2.

The exterior is coated with black varnish, and a red filling ring is stencilled round the head.

The **Mark II bomb** differs from the Mark I in not being fitted with a parachute, also in a slight rearrangement of the internal filling; the bottom of the body is closed with a millboard disc, secured by a covering of shellaced brown paper.

The **Mark III bomb** (Plate V) differs from the Mark II in having the smoke composition mixed with 10 per cent. of special aluminium powder, and the two powder puffs contain larger charges of igniting composition.

BOMB, 3·45-INCH, PARACHUTE, FLARE.

The **Mark I bomb** is generally similar in construction to the Mark I signal smoke bomb (page 1), but the body is longer, is filled with four aluminium stars, 7-grain powder puff, and a Japanese silk parachute, and is closed at the bottom by a wood plug tacked in.

The **Mark II bomb** differs from the Mark I in having a 50-grain powder puff, in the quickmatch being shorter, and the base being closed by a tinned plate cup secured by three copper tacks clenched over.

The **Mark III bomb** differs from the Mark II in having a 40-grain powder puff and a slightly modified form of parachute upon which the word "BRITISH" is stencilled in black.

The **Mark IV bomb** differs from the Mark II in the head being secured to the body by riveting and soldering the tin cup instead of being secured by copper tacks, and in the wood block being affixed in the head with Pettman cement.

The **Mark V bomb** (Plate VI) differs from the Mark IV in having the tin cup secured to the base by bayonet joints instead of by copper tacks, three brass rivets being soldered to the cup to engage in slots cut in the body; the joints are covered by strips of white paper secured by shellac. The wood strips for packing between the stars are larger, and the powder puff contains a charge of 28 grains instead of 50 grains of R. P. powder.

BOMB, 3·45-INCH, RECONNAISSANCE, FLARE, MARK I, 9-SECS. DELAY.

This bomb (Plate VII) is generally similar in construction to the Mark V parachute flare bomb (*see* page 2) differing in dimensions of candles and body, also in being fitted with a delay which is formed by the insertion of a coil of safety fuze between the electric tube and the detonator holder, the latter containing a " delay " pellet instead of an ordinary powder pellet.

The exterior of the bomb, with the exception of the electric contact strips, is painted green, a red ring being stencilled round the head to denote that the bomb is filled. In addition the words "Opens after dropping 1,000 feet" are stencilled in red on the side and a descriptive label is gummed on immediately below the red ring.

BOMB, TRIPLE FLARE, MARK I, 12-SECS, 6-SECS., AND 2½-SECS. DELAY.

This bomb (Plate VIII) consists of three paper cylinders containing flare composition, paper cylinder containing friction fuze ignition arrangement, and parachute.

The flare composition cylinders, which are secured together by two calico bands, are covered with calico, which is tied at one end round strings connected with a spring hook to which the strings of the parachute are attached, and at the other end round the safety fuze projecting from the cylinder containing the friction ignition arrangement, the length of the safety fuze being regulated by the delay provided for (either 12, 6, or 2½ seconds).

The friction fuze ignition arrangement consists of quickmatch contained in a paper cylinder, the lower end of which is coated internally with friction composition; the whole is contained in an outer cylinder with a band of calico round the bottom, by which the cylinder is secured to the safety fuze connected with the flare cylinder. A string is tied round the friction fuze and passed through a slot in the outer cylinder, a spring swivel hook being tied on the end.

A cord with ring attached is tied round the body of the bomb just below the outer cylinder of the friction fuze.

MARKING.—The upper calico band binding the three flare cylinders is painted red, and the body is coated with aluminium paint. A label is also affixed stating the delay embodied in the bomb.

Bombs, 4.

The **parachute** is 50 inches in diameter and is made of black sateen lined with silvered tissue paper. It is folded up and secured by a paper band, which is broken before inserting in the dropping tube.

The word "BRITISH" is stencilled on the parachute.

BOMBS, 4·2-INCH, SIGNAL, COLOURED SMOKE, MARK I.

This **bomb** (Plate IX) consists of a cylindrical body containing 14 coloured smoke candles and a bursting charge, and fitted with a striking arrangement on the top.

The body is made of tinned plate, closed at the top with a soldered-on cap having a screwed spigot in the centre to receive the striking arrangement and igniter. It is closed at the bottom by a tinned plate cover secured by an adhesive tape band, and is filled as follows:—

A cardboard disc primed with priming paste and F.G. powder and layers of quickmatch is placed in the end next the spigot and two tiers of coloured smoke candles (14 in all) assembled below. The candles are each contained in an aluminium case, powder coated, and have four holes (two in the side and one in the top and bottom) which are filled with quickmatch and priming.

A felt wad is placed between the candles and the bottom of the bomb and cotton wool is placed round the candles to form a tight package.

The igniter consists of a shortened ·410 Eley sporting cartridge fitted with a perforated brass cup to which is attached a ·8-inch length of No. 16 Bickford safety fuze. The striking arrangement consists of a cylindrical brass chamber containing a steel striker and spring, brass release pin and safety pin.

The brass chamber is enlarged in diameter and screwed at one end to suit the spigot on the body of the bomb, and has a hole at the other end through which the top end of the striker protrudes. A hole is bored in opposite sides to receive the safety pin.

The striker has a point formed at one end, also a flange which forms a shoulder for the spring. The other end is radiused outwards and bored down the centre, four slots being cut down the side about 1·125-inches long to permit of the end being sprung open by the insertion of the releasing pin, to grip on the edge of the hole in the top of the striker chamber. The striker is actuated by a spring held in compression between the flange on the head of the striker and the top of the striker chamber.

The releasing pin is made of brass, tapered off below a rounded head through which a becket is passed connecting it to the safety pin.

ACTION.— On removal of the safety and releasing pins, the striker spring asserts itself, driving the striker forward and firing the igniter, the flash from which ignites the bursting charge, thus blowing the candles out of the bottom.

The candles are ignited by means of the priming with which they are coated and by the quickmatch in the holes.

MARKING.— The bombs, which may be filled with either red, blue, yellow or purple smoke candles, or combinations of these colours, are painted a drab colour and have coloured serpentine lines stencilled round the side to denote the colour or combination of colours.

BOMB, 4·5-INCH, SIGNAL, SMOKE, MARK I.

The **bomb** (Plate X) consists of a cylindrical paper body, three smoke candles, opening charge in paper bag, friction igniter and strawboard discs.

The bomb is assembled in the following manner:—

A strawboard disc is placed in the bottom of the paper body and the three smoke candles loaded in on top and securely held in position by paper packing. Over the smoke candles is placed the opening charge of 2 ozs. of coarse black powder contained in a paper bag which is primed on the outer top surface with mealed powder. The mouth of the bomb is then closed with two discs of strawboard, glued in, each perforated with a central hole into which is glued the friction igniter.

The smoke candles are each made up with a rolled paper cylinder filled with smoke composition and closed at both ends with a layer of clay. Four holes are pierced in the side of the cylinder into which are inserted lengths of quickmatch, the free ends of which are carried up the side, tied on top, and prevented from becoming detached by means of a strip of brown paper glued round the candle.

The friction igniter consists of a length of calico covered quickmatch fitted at the lower end into a paper cylinder having a ·5-inch length of firework fuze in the lower portion, and secured by means of a calico cover choked round the quickmatch with string. The upper end of the quickmatch is coated with igniting composition and fitted with a calico-covered cylindrical paper sleeve coated internally at the bottom with friction composition and secured by choking with string.

During transit the free end of the igniter is turned over and held against the side of the bomb by a rubber band.

ACTION.—The rubber band is removed and the sleeve pulled smartly away, the friction composition in the sleeve igniting that on the end of the quickmatch. The quickmatch burns until it reaches the firework fuze, the flash from which ignites the opening charge, the smoke candles becoming ignited by means of the quickmatch leading into the holes in the side.

MARKING.—The exterior of the bomb is painted with black shellac varnish, and has a ·5-inch red ring painted round the body near the head denoting that it is filled. A label with the name of the bomb printed on it is gummed to the side.

BOMB, GROUND FLARE.

The **Mark I bomb** (Plate XI) consists of a cylindrical sheet zinc body closed at the bottom with a cup disc and fitted with a pointed cast-iron nose. The body is filled with flare mixture primed at the top with priming mixture, F.G. powder and quickmatch, and is closed at the tail by a perforated steel disc which rests on a ring of tinned-iron wire soldered into the body, the rear end of the body being spun over the disc to secure it.

A **fuze, bomb, tail, No. 26, Mark I** (described below), having a cambric parachute attached to it by a wire loop is sweated on to the steel disc over the central perforation, and a cylindrical tinned plate cap is placed over the fuze and rear end of the body and secured by a strip of adhesive tape wound round the junction.

A brass lug is riveted to the body at about the centre of gravity of the bomb for attachment to the releasing gear of the bomb-dropping apparatus, and a wire loop and whipcord becket is attached to the head of the cap. The safety pin of the fuze is passed through corresponding holes in the cap.

The fuze consists of a brass body with cap chamber, check pins and springs, striker pin and spring, collar and safety pin.

The body is cylindrical in shape and is reduced in diameter above the base; it is bored out internally, screwed at the base to receive the cap chamber, and has four longitudinal sawcuts made in the rear end. Bulges are formed internally and externally near the end, the internal bulge to grip under a shoulder formed on the striker pin, the external bulge being gripped by the collar thus holding the striker spring in compression between the internal bulge in the body and the head of the striker.

Corresponding holes are drilled diametrically through the collar, body, and striker pin, to receive a steel safety pin, and two holes are bored through the body immediately below the striker head for the inserting of the check pins and springs. The check pins are retained in position by the walls of the rear cap which is placed over the body of the bomb. A shortened Eley's ·410 sporting cartridge is placed in the recess in the cap chamber.

ACTION.—The adhesive tape at the junction of the bomb body and cap and the safety pin having been removed the bomb is released. The weight of the body withdraws it from the cap which is left suspended on the dropping gear by the whipcord becket. The action of the bomb withdrawing from the cap allows the springs behind the check pins to assert themselves and force the latter clear of the fuze. On impact the nose of the bomb embeds itself into the ground and the retaining collar of the fuze moves downwards, releasing its grip round the bulge in the body, whereupon the striker is forced downwards by the spring on to the Eley cartridge, the flash from which ignites the priming in the bomb and fires the flare mixture, the flare issuing through the perforations in the rear closing disc.

MARKING.—The body is painted drab, the nose and cap green, and a ·25-inch red band is stencilled round the cap near the base.

BOMB, MESSAGE CARRYING, AERIAL, MARK I.

The **bomb** (Plate XII) consists of a steel cylinder 5·95 inches long, ·942-inch diameter with a striking arrangement sweated on to one side.

The cylinder is turned in at the base over a steel disc and closed at the top by a perforated steel plug secured by crimping the mouth of the cylinder into a groove formed in the plug; the perforation in the plug is covered with a disc of shellaced paper. Two holes are drilled in the sides, one below the head to receive the end of the igniter (described below) and one diametrically opposite the striking arrangement, the latter hole being filled with fusible solder.

The cylinder is filled with smoke mixture and primed with match composition.

. The striking arrangement consists of a brass body, steel striker, striker spring, releasing lever, safety pin and ring.

The body is bored out to receive the striker and spring, and threaded at the mouth to receive a screwed bush which retains the igniter (described below) in position.

The head of the striker protrudes through a hole in the top of the body and is retained in position by one end of a bent lever on the outside, two lugs on the top of the body being notched to receive the fulcrum flanges on the lever. Two holes are drilled diametrically through the body immediately below the head of the striker to receive the safety pin.

Bombs, 8.

The **igniter** consists of a cut down ·410 Eley sporting cartridge pressed into two perforated brass cups covered with a paper protector, and a 2·1-inch length of No. 15 or 15A safety fuze which is secured by six small spikes formed on the inner cup.

The head of the igniter is placed in the mouth of the striking arrangement and secured by the screwed bush and the free end of the safety fuze is inserted into the hole below the head of the smoke cylinder.

The **container** is made of linen or calico 21·375 inches long by 6·5 inches wide and has a pocket formed at each end, one being left open to receive the bomb and the other, into which the message is inserted, lined with asbestos and provided with a flap secured by means of a press stud. Eyeletted holes are made for the reception of the safety pin.

The bomb is inserted into the open pocket of the container with the fulcrum and lever projecting through a hole in the side, the container being wrapped round so that the lever is immediately secured. A rubber band is placed round the container to prevent it unwrapping and an instruction label is affixed to the outside of the message pocket.

INSTRUCTIONS FOR FIRING.

The rubber band is removed, care being taken that the container does not become unwrapped, the message is inserted into the pocket and the flap closed. The safety pin is then removed and the bomb and container thrown overboard.

ACTION.—After the bomb is thrown, the container becomes unwrapped, releasing the lever, which drops away and thus allows the striker spring to assert itself and drive the striker on to the head of the igniter and fire the smoke composition in the cylinder.

CANDLE, SMOKE, GROUND.

The **Mark I candle** (Plate XIII) consists of a cylindrical tinned iron case filled with smoke composition, with a friction arrangement on the top covered with paper.

The firing arrangement consists of a black blob of friction composition with touch paper, priming composition, and quickmatch underneath. A tear-off strip having attached to it a tin cap to cover the blob of friction composition, and a cardboard disc covered with striking mixture, is secured across the top and fastened down at the side of the candle.

The exterior of the candle is painted with black shellac paint, and a label giving designation of the candle and instructions for use is pasted over the top of the body.

The **Mark II candle** (Plate XIII) differs from the **Mark I** in the case being made of IXX tin, and in having a spring-on tin lid with a central hole, through which protrudes a tin thimble containing the blob of friction composition. The blob of friction composition is larger, and the priming underneath is slightly different.

The directions for firing are placed on the side.

CARTRIDGE, ILLUMINATING, 1½-INCH PARACHUTE.

The **Mark I** (Plate XIV) **cartridge** consists of an empty case with primer, propelling charge, and a cylinder containing a white illuminating star, parachute and ejecting charge.

The case consists of a brown paper cylinder with a brass base having a central hole to receive the primer, and fitted internally with a stiffening cylinder of No. 37 S.W.G. sheet steel and a compressed paper or strawboard wad.

The primer is made of brass, recessed at the base and fitted with a percussion cap, and the magazine is filled with about 8 grains of R.P. powder.

The star and parachute, connected by an asbestos cord, are contained in a brown paper cylinder closed at the top with a pasted-on calico band and at the bottom with a wood block glued in, a perforated felt wad and cardboard disc being secured to the lower face of the block by 3 copper brads. A perforated felt wad is placed below the star, and the cavity between this wad and the top surface of the block is filled with an ejecting charge of about 10 grains of loose powder, a recess in the top of the block being primed with mealed powder.

The cylinder is placed in the case over a propelling charge of about 123 grains of R.F.G.[2] powder, and a 1·2-inch length of safety fuze is passed through a central hole in the wood block connecting the propelling charge to the ejecting charge in the star cylinder.

ACTION.—On firing the pistol, the flash from the primer ignites the charge in the base, propelling the cylinder from the case and igniting the safety fuze in the wood block. The safety fuze burns until it reaches the charge, above the wood block, which bursts and ejects the star and parachute from the top of the cylinder, the star becoming ignited by strands of quickmatch led through the bottom.

The **Mark II cartridge** (Plate XV) differs from the Mark I in being fitted at the base with a cap chamber and percussion cap instead of a primer.

The top of the cylinder may be closed with a tinned plate cap instead of the wood head.

The **Mark III cartridge** (Plate XV) differs from the Mark II in the cylinder for the parachute and star being shorter and closed by cardboard discs which are held in place by the mouth of the cartridge case being turned over. The parachute is folded round a cylindrical paper core and a cardboard diaphragm is placed between the parachute and star which are connected by copper wire instead of asbestos cord.

The above-mentioned cartridges have a white label attached bearing the words "White Parachute Cartridge."

CARTRIDGE, ILLUMINATING, 1½-INCH, DARK IGNITION.

The **Mark I cartridge** (Plate XVI) consists of an empty case and primer (made up similarly to that described for the 1½-inch parachute cartridge on page 10), filled with a charge of 123 grains of R.F.G.^{2} powder and a white illuminating star separated by a perforated felt wad and cardboard disc. The star is held firmly in position by a felt wad and cardboard disc placed over the top, and the mouth of the cartridge is closed by two cardboard discs shellaced in.

The star consists of an aluminium cylinder having the upper portion filled with light composition and the lower portion primed with mealed powder and quickmatch, the latter being led through a hole in the cylinder and connected to the propelling charge in the cartridge.

A white label bearing the words " Illuminating, Dark Ignition " is pasted on the outside of the closing disc for identification purposes.

The **Mark II cartridge** differs from the Mark I in the case being fitted with a cap chamber and percussion cap instead of a primer, and in the closing disc, which may be made of cardboard or tinned or coppered plate, being secured in position by the mouth of the case being turned in. A cylindrical brown paper distance piece is placed between the closing disc and the disc over the star.

CARTRIDGES, ILLUMINATING, 1-INCH.

The **Mark I cartridge** (Plate XVII) is made up similarly to the Mark II 1½-inch dark ignition cartridge (*see* above) except that the case is made of brass with a paper lining instead of paper with brass base, and the star is primed at both ends instead of only the bottom end. The space between the closing disc and the wad over the star is filled with cardboard discs instead of a distance piece.

A circular white label bearing the words " Illuminating, Dark Ignition " is pasted on the top of the closing disc for identification purposes.

The **Mark II cartridge** differs from the Mark I in having a paper case with brass base.

CARTRIDGES, SIGNAL, 1½-INCH, WHITE.

The **Mark I cartridge** (Plate XVIII) consists of an empty case and primer (similar to those described on page 10), filled with a charge of about 40 grains R.F.G.2 powder and a white signal star separated by a perforated felt wad and cardboard disc. The star is held firmly in position by a cardboard disc placed over the top, and the mouth of the cartridge is closed by two cardboard discs shellaced in.

The star consists of a cylindrical aluminium case filled with signal composition primed at each end with mealed powder. Both ends of the cylinder have a central perforation through which is led a length of quickmatch, and the upper end of the star is primed externally with mealed powder and connected to the lower priming by a narrow coating of F.G. powder secured down the side of the star.

A circular white label bearing the words "Aircraft, white" is gummed to the outside of the closing disc and the mouth of the case is painted white for a depth of ½-inch for identification purposes.

In addition, half the circumference of the base is milled in order to distinguish the colour by touch in the dark. This milling will, however, be omitted in future supplies.

The **Mark II cartridge** differs from the Mark I in the case being fitted with a cap chamber and percussion cap instead of a primer, and in the closing disc, which may be made of cardboard or tinned or coppered plate, being secured in position by the mouth of the case being turned in. A cylindrical brown paper distance piece is placed between the closing disc and the disc over the star.

CARTRIDGES, SIGNAL, 1½-INCH { RED GREEN YELLOW } **WITHOUT SMOKE.**

These **cartridges** (Plate XIX) are made up similarly to the Mark II 1½-inch white signal cartridge described above except that the star is made up in a calico bag choked at both ends with twine, and primed with quickmatch. The bag and twine is of the same colour as the star and the end of the cartridge is coloured for a distance of ·25-inch from the mouth.

A circular label of the same colour as the star is pasted on the closing disc of the cartridge, or alternatively a white label bearing the words "Red," "Green," or "Yellow" in their respective colours, may be used. In addition the circumference of the base of the cartridge is milled in order that the colour of the star may be distinguished by touch, viz., milled all round for the red star, in four equal distant spaces for the yellow star, whilst for the green star the edge is left plain. This milling will, however be omitted in future supplies.

CARTRIDGES, SIGNAL, 1½-INCH { GREEN / RED } WITH SMOKE.

The **Mark I cartridge** (Plate XX) differ from the cartridge without smoke described above in being made up with a case and primer as described on page 10, and in a charge of smoke composition being inserted in the top of the calico bag containing the star.

The **Mark II cartridge** (Plate XXI) differ from the Mark I in being made up in a case fitted with cap chamber and percussion cap instead of the primer.

The cartridges are distinguished by the mouth of the case being coloured and by a green or red label on the closing disc bearing the word "Aircraft." The base may also be milled as described for the signal cartridges without smoke (page 12) but this method of identification will be omitted in future supplies.

CARTRIDGES, SIGNAL, 1½-INCH, PARACHUTE, CHANGING { RED / WHITE TO GREEN } MARK I.

These **cartridges** (Plate XXII) are made up similarly to the Mark III illuminating cartridge described on page 11 differing only in the star being filled with white and red, or white and green composition.

The cartridges may be distinguished by the following markings.

A circular label of white paper bearing an appropriately coloured concentric disc is attached to the closing disc by shellac, the words "White to Red" or "White to Green," as the case may be, are printed in white on the coloured disc, and the words "Parachute cartridge" are printed in the same colour as the star (*i.e.*, red or green), on the white portion of the label. Two coloured bands each ½-inch in width are painted round the mouth of the cartridge, the band nearest the mouth being white and the lower one either red or green according to the colour of the star.

CARTRIDGES, SIGNAL, 1½-INCH, WITH PARACHUTE AND COLOURED SMOKE.

The **Mark I cartridge** (Plate XXIII) consists of an empty case made up in a similar manner to that described for the 1½-inch Mark II dark ignition cartridge (page 11) filled with a propelling charge of two drams R.F.G.[1] powder over which is placed a millboard washer and perforated felt disc. A cardboard cylinder, containing the smoke star and parachute is placed over the felt disc and secured into the case by a band of adhesive calico wound round the mouth of the latter.

The parachute and star are contained in the cylinder in a similar manner to that described on page 10 for the Mark I 1½-inch illuminating cartridge, except that the head of the cylinder is closed with a wood head secured by a band of adhesive paper, and a ·812-inch length of No. 14 Bickford fuze is placed in the central hole in the wood plug at the base.

The star may contain either yellow, blue or purple or red smoke mixture, and a white label bearing the words "Parachute smoke signal, Red" (or such other colour as may be appropriate) is attached to the cylinder for identification purposes. In addition the wood head and paper securing band on the head will be painted to correspond with the colour of the star.

The **Mark II cartridge** (Plate XXIV) differs from the Mark I in being made up in a longer case in which the cylinder containing the star and parachute is enclosed. The cartridge is closed by turning in the mouth of the case on to a cap of tinned or coppered plate, the wooden head in the star and parachute cylinder being omitted.

The smoke star is slightly different in construction, consisting of a cylindrical tube of paper closed at each end with a perforated wood plug filled with a perforated pellet of yellow, blue, purple or red smoke mixture, the perforations in the plugs and pellet being filled with powder.

The ends of the star and a length along each side are coated with priming, and the star is bound externally with copper wire to which the cord of the parachute is attached.

CARTRIDGE, SIGNAL, 1½-INCH, WITH CHANGING COLOUR STAR.

The **Mark I cartridge** (Plate XXV) consists of an empty case with cap and cap chamber similar to that described for the Mark II 1½-inch white signal cartridge (page 12) filled with a charge of 32 grains R.F.G.^{2} powder, over which are placed, in the order named, a perforated strawboard disc and felt wad, star, strawboard disc and cylindrical paper distance piece, the cartridge being closed by a strawboard or tinned or coppered sheet disc placed over the distance piece and secured by turning in the mouth of the case.

The star consists of a paper cylinder closed at the top with a strawboard wad, below which is a layer of clay, two layers of colour composition and one of priming mixture. Coloured paper strips are pasted round the star to denote colours.

The cartridges are made up with combinations of red, green, and white composition, and the combination is denoted by two coloured bands painted round the mouth of the cartridge.

CARTRIDGES, SIGNAL, 1½-INCH, THREE STAR, DARK IGNITION.

The **Mark I cartridge** (Plate XXVI) consists of a cylindrical brown paper case with brass base, fitted with cap chamber and percussion cap and filled with a charge of R.F.G.² powder and a paper cylinder containing the stars.

The star cylinder is separated from the charge by a perforated felt wad between two perforated cardboard discs and is held in position by a felt wad placed over the top, the mouth of the cartridge being closed by turning in over a cardboard disc. Alternatively a cylindrical paper distance piece may be placed over the cylinder and the mouth of the cartridge closed by turning in over a tinned or coppered sheet disc.

The cylinder contains three stars (red, green, and yellow) made up in paper tubes each having suitably coloured paper pasted round to indicate the nature of the star. Similar bands are also pasted round the cylinder.

The two lower stars are perforated to receive a length of quickmatch below which is a cardboard disc primed on both sides.

The star cylinder is closed at the top by a cardboard disc and at the bottom by a perforated wood plug glued in, through which is inserted a short length of safety fuze communicating with the propelling charge.

A black ring is painted round the top of the cartridge and three coloured discs on the side to indicate the colours of the stars contained.

The **Mark II cartridge** differs from the Mark I in being made up with a solid drawn brass case, with a brown paper lining.

Cartridges, 16.

CARTRIDGE, SIGNAL, 1½-INCH, PARACHUTE REDUCED CHARGE.

The **Mark I cartridge** differs from the cartridge illuminating, parachute, 1½-inch, Mark III (page 10) in containing a reduced propelling charge.

The letter "A" in 1-inch type is stencilled on the side of the case and also on the closing disc.

CARTRIDGES, SIGNAL, 1½-INCH, WITH SCINTILLATING STAR.

The **Mark I cartridge** (Plate XXVII) is made up in similar manner to the 1½-inch red signal cartridge without smoke (page 12) but it is fitted with a scintillating star, and the distance piece is omitted.

The star consists of a cylindrical charge of scintillating mixture covered with calico, the top and bottom and a length on each side primed with paste, the calico bag and quickmatch as in the red signal cartridge being omitted.

A white wavy band is painted round near the mouth of the cartridge and a paper label giving the designation of the cartridge is pasted on the closing disc.

The **Mark II cartridge** differs from the Mark I in having a solid drawn brass case lined with a brown paper cylinder.

CARTRIDGES, SIGNAL, 1-INCH, AIRCRAFT WHITE.

The **Mark I cartridge** (Plate XXVIII) consists of a charge of loose powder and a signal star contained in a paper-lined solid drawn brass case, fitted with a cap chamber and cap. The star consists of an aluminium cylinder with partly closed ends, containing signal composition, primed at each end with mealed powder and quickmatch. A perforated felt wad is placed between the charge and star, and a cardboard disc and distance piece on top of the star. The cartridge is closed by a cardboard, or tinned or coppered sheet disc placed over the distance piece and secured by the mouth of the case being turned in.

The **Mark II cartridge** differs from the Mark I in having a paper case with brass base instead of a solid drawn brass case with paper lining.

The cartridges are distinguished by the case being painted white at the mouth and by a label bearing the words "Aircraft white" which is pasted on the closing disc.

CARTRIDGES, SIGNAL, 1-INCH, BLACK STREAMER.

The **Mark I cartridge** (Plate XXIX) consists of a paper case with brass base, similar to that described above for the Mark II aircraft signal cartridge, containing a charge of 33 grains of loose powder, above which are placed a felt wad between two cardboard wads, and the black streamer. The streamer consists of a 66-inch length of 4·1-inch width satin-like material wound round a wooden stick and having a strip of lead sewn into one end.

The cartridge is closed in a similar manner to the Mark I aircraft white cartridge.

The **Mark II cartridge** differs from the Mark I in having a solid drawn brass case as described above for the Mark I aircraft white cartridge.

The cartridges have a label bearing the words "Black streamer" pasted on to the closing disc.

CARTRIDGES, SIGNAL, 1-INCH, GREEN, RED, WHITE, AND YELLOW.

The **Mark IV cartridges** (Plate XXX) which differ from each other only in the colour of composition in the star, consist of a case, cap, chamber and cap as fitted to the Mark I aircraft white cartridge described on page 16 containing a charge of loose powder and a signal star.

The star consists of a calico wrapper containing either red, green, white, or yellow composition (as the case may be) primed with quickmatch, the ends of the wrapper being choked with string. Perforated wads of felt and cardboard are placed between the charge and star and a perforated felt wad is placed on top of the star. Cardboard discs, as necessary to make a tight package, are placed over the felt wad and the cartridge is closed by the mouth being turned in.

The **Mark V cartridges** differ from the Mark IV in having a paper case with brass base instead of the paper lined solid drawn brass case as fitted to the latter.

Cartridges, 18.

The cartridges have the case painted near the mouth with a colour corresponding to that of the star and have a label bearing the words " Red," "Green," " White," or " Yellow " as appropriate, pasted on to the closing discs.

In addition to the above markings, Naval Service red and white cartridges have the rim of case milled in order that the cartridges may be distinguished in the dark, the white cartridge being milled half round the base and the red cartridge right round; the green cartridge is left plain.

Later supplies of the above Marks IV and V cartridges (in Land Service only) will have a paper distance piece inserted above the star and the upper felt wad omitted.

FLARE, GROUND, ½-HOUR, RED.

The **Mark I flare** (Plate XXXI) consists of a paper cylinder closed at the bottom by a calico disc, and secured into a cylindrical paper socket filled with plaster of paris, into which is embedded a 6-inch commercial wire nail, which protrudes from the bottom to form a spike.

The body is filled with red flare composition and is closed at the head by an igniter formed with two discs of cardboard, the lower disc being perforated and the recess thus formed filled with match top composition.

A tear-off band, to which is attached a cardboard disc, covered with amorphous striking mixture, is affixed between the two cardboard discs and the free end secured to the side of the body.

To ignite the flare the tear-off tape is pulled sharply upwards, thus removing the top cardboard disc and baring the igniter, which is then ignited by rubbing the amorphous disc sharply across the match top composition.

A red label, giving the designation of the flare and instructions for use, is pasted over the top of the body.

FLARES, GROUND, $\begin{cases} 3 \text{ inches} \times 2 \text{ inches} \\ 1\frac{3}{4} \text{ ,, } \times 2 \text{ ,, } \\ 1\frac{1}{2} \text{ ,, } \times 1\frac{1}{2} \text{ ,, } \end{cases}$ $\begin{cases} \text{RED.} \\ \text{GREEN.} \\ \text{YELLOW.} \\ \text{WHITE.} \end{cases}$

These flares (Plate XXXII) differ from the ½-hour flare described above in not being fitted with the socket containing plaster of paris and nail, also in dimensions. A paper direction label, the colour of which corresponds to the colour of the composition in the flare, is pasted on the top of each flare.

FLARES, SIGNAL, $\begin{cases} \text{RED.} \\ \text{GREEN.} \end{cases}$

The **Mark I flares** (Plate XXXIII) consist of a paper cylinder containing light composition secured to a wood handle. Igniting composition is placed on top of the light composition and the cylinder closed by a cardboard disc and paper cap. A cardboard cap with igniting composition on the bottom of the inside, is secured on the end of the handle by a lead capsule. The paper cap with cardboard disc and lead capsule are each removed by a tear-off tape when the flares are required for use.

Instructions for use are contained on the label attached to the flares.

FLARES, LANDING:—

One minute, Mark I.—
Red tint.
Deep red.

Two minute, Mark I.—
Red tint.
Deep red.

The **one-minute flares** (Plate XXXIV) consist of a cylindrical paper case covered with tinfoil and calico, closed at one end with a perforated wood block cemented in, and at the other end with a tinfoil cap. A paper central tube is fitted into the hole in the wood block and closed at the top with a small perforated wood plug, two electric leads being inserted through this perforation and attached to a No. 22 electric igniter placed at the opposite end of the central tube. The two wire leads are secured by the calico covering of the body being chocked round them with thread.

The igniter is surrounded by a layer of priming and strands of quickmatch, and the space between the central tube and the body is filled with red tinted or deep red flare composition as applicable.

The **two-minute flares** are made up similarly to the one-minute flares described above, but are longer.

A label giving the designation, colour, and instructions for fixing is attached to the end which fits into the holder.

A number of the flares were issued with labels bearing the words "Holt landing light flare, Mark II, PAT.," but later supplies bear the designation as shown above.

The flares are carried on night-flying aircraft for assistance to the pilot in landing, and are inserted into special holders fitted to the wing tips or tail booms of the craft.

GRENADES, ·303-INCH RIFLE, NO. 31, DAYLIGHT SIGNAL.

The **Mark I** was allocated to a design of grenade of which only a small number were made and none of which have been issued to the Service.

The **Mark II grenade** (Plate XXXV) consists of a cylindrical body of IXX tinned plate with a No. 24 S.W.G. tin plate lid soldered on, the lid being fitted with a threaded boss to receive the striking arrangement. The base cover of the grenade is dished and is a sliding fit on the body; a metal tube is soldered to the interior of the base cover to form a centring piece, and a steel base bored out and screwed to receive a 15-inch steel rod is soldered to the under surface.

The striker chamber is tubular, enlarged at the base to form a chamber for the head of the igniter and is threaded for a portion of its length to suit the screwed boss on the head of the grenade. Two holes are drilled in the side to form a gas escape.

The striker consists of a cylindrical bar of brass with a projection at one end, and it is held in position over the igniter by a copper shearing wire which is passed through holes drilled in the striker and striker chamber and the ends twisted together. A brass cover is secured over the striker chamber and a safety pin is passed through corresponding holes in the cover, striker chamber and striker. This safety pin is only removed just prior to the grenade being fired from the rifle.

The grenade is filled in the following manner:

Under the head is placed a felt wad perforated in the centre and primed on its upper surface with one dram of F.G. powder. Four lengths of quickmatch are led from under the igniter (described below) through the felt wad and into the smoke composition candle. A wooden diaphragm placed under the candle has a slot cut in the side through which is passed a strip of asbestos cord connecting the candle to a rice-paper parachute, which is folded up and placed round a cylindrical paper tube, the latter being retained in its central position by the metal tube in the base cover. Any space between the body and candle or parachute is filled with packing.

The smoke candle, which may be either red, blue, yellow or purple has a half-inch patch painted on the side to denote colour of composition, and the body of the grenade is painted drab colour with serpentine coloured lines stencilled on to indicate the colour of the candle contained.

The parachutes fitted to Naval Service grenades have the word "BRITISH" stencilled on them in 1-inch black letters.

Grenades, 22.

The igniter consists of an Eley ·410-inch cartridge cut down and pressed on to a length of No. 15 A. safety fuze. It is placed in the tube in the grenade before firing, the striker chamber being unscrewed and a damp proof disc, which is secured over the boss, torn off.

ACTION.—After inserting the igniter and removing the safety pin and cover from the striker, the grenade is placed in position with the rod in the rifle. The striker is then struck smartly on the head and the rifle fired. When the striker is hit the shearing wire breaks and the striker point impales the head of the igniter, the flash from which after a short delay ignites the quickmatch and powder priming in the head of the grenade, the priming ejecting the candle and parachute from the base of the grenade, and the quickmatch burning until it reaches the smoke candle and ignites it.

The **Mark III grenade** (Plate XXXVI) differs from the Mark II in the following particulars:—

The candles are fitted with wood plugs at each end, the calico band being omitted; they are bound with soft iron wire to which the parachute cord is attached.

The blue candle has priming holes ·25-inch diameter bored at each end to which the quickmatch is led, and it is suspended from the side.

The other candles are suspended from one end, the purple one having a ·25-inch priming hole at the opposite end and another hole ·1875-inch diameter through the centre.

The red and yellow candles have a single hole through the centre into which the quickmatch is led.

Ordinary thick cord may be used for suspending the candle instead of asbestos cord.

The diaphragm consists of a felt wad attached to a cardboard disc instead of wood. A cylindrical distance piece of cardboard with felt washer at the base is used in place of the paper tube, the parachute being folded round the exterior of the distance piece and the cord coiled inside.

A coloured paper band is pasted round the bottom of the stars instead of the painted patch but the body of the grenade is marked in a similar manner to the Mark II.

GRENADES, ·303-INCH RIFLE, No. 32.

The **Mark I** was assigned to a design of grenade of which only a small number were made and of which none were issued to the Service.

The **Mark II grenade** (Plate XXXVII) differs from the Mark II, No. 31, grenade described on page 21 in being fitted with a combination of either two or three coloured illuminating stars. When two stars are fitted, a dummy star is placed in position to make a tight package.

The stars may contain red, green, or yellow illuminating composition and have a half-inch patch, corresponding to the colour of the composition, painted on the side.

The body of the grenade is painted drab colour, and has coloured dots painted on the side to show the colour and order of the stars. These dots are so placed that when the grenade is in position for firing, the sequence of stars is indicated as they will appear after the parachute has opened.

The **Mark III grenade** (Plate XXXVIII) differs from the Mark II in having the stars fitted with a shorter length of quickmatch and wood plugs in the head, to which the asbestos cord is attached instead of the calico bands, which are omitted. Ordinary thick cord may be used for suspending the stars, and the diaphragm is made of cardboard instead of wood.

The colour of the stars is indicated by a paper band round the base of the star or by a coloured paper case, the body of the grenade being painted and marked in a similiar manner to the Mark II grenade.

The parachute is made of Japanese or other suitable paper instead of rice paper.

GRENADE, ·303-INCH RIFLE, No. 38.

No "**Mark I**" grenades have been made.

The "**Mark II**" grenade (Plate XXXIX) is similiar to the No. 32 Mark II grenade described above but differs in having a circular instead of an octagonal parachute and in the signal consisting of a single star changing colour from white to red and back to white, or red to green and back to red as ordered. The head of the star is closed by a felt wad and cardboard disc with central hole for the cord attaching it to the parachute. The bottom is closed by a paper cover. The star has three paper bands, one red between two white or one green between two red, pasted round the body. Similar bands are painted round the body of the grenade to indicate colour and order of the star enclosed.

Grenades, 24.

GRENADE, ·303-INCH RIFLE, No. 42, DAY SIGNAL.

The **Mark I grenade** (Plate XL) consists of a rolled paper cylinder closed at the base with a wood block and at the head with a dished tin plate cap, containing a coloured smoke candle (yellow, purple, red or blue) and a parachute. A supporting collar of black or tinned plate which fits the mouth of the discharger is secured round the body near the head by adhesive tape.

The wood block in the base is covered on the outside by a brass cap embossed in the centre to receive a steel disc to prevent the wood being burnt by the flash of the propellant and has two holes through it lengthways to contain fuze which conveys the flash of the propelling charge to a felt wad primed on its underside with gunpowder, and having five strands of quickmatch led through a central hole and splayed out on the top side next to the candle.

The yellow, purple and red candles consist of a rolled paper case containing the smoke composition, closed at each end by a wood plug having a central hole through which quickmatch is passed up through the centre of the composition. One end of the candle is primed and covered with paper, and the two wood plugs at the ends are connected by a binding wire.

The blue candle is made up similarly to the other colours except that the quickmatch is not passed up through the centre of the candle but down the side, and there is no priming at one end.

A 3-feet length of asbestos or other suitable cord is bound round the body of the candle and attached to the parachute so that the candle will be suspended horizontally. A cardboard disc is threaded on this cord so that it comes between the star and the parachute when assembled in the grenades.

The parachute, which is filled up and assembled in the top of the grenade, is octagonal in shape and made of Japanese or other suitable paper; strong thread is secured to each corner and brought together and tied to the asbestos cord of the candle.

A serpentine line about 3 inches long is painted on the side of the body indicating the colour of smoke produced by the candle, and a paper label giving the designation of the grenade is pasted on the head.

GRENADE, ·303-INCH RIFLE, No. 45, NIGHT SIGNAL.

The **Mark I grenade** (Plate XLI) is made up similarly to the No. 42 described above, differing in being fitted with a changing colour star instead of a smoke candle

The star consists of a rolled paper case containing a charge of star composition of three colours with priming at the bottom; it is suspended from the head.

Three paper bands showing the colours and sequence of the composition are pasted round the body of the star.

The colours of the stars in the sequence they will appear, when the parachute has opened, are also painted as a 2-inch square on the body of the grenade.

GRENADE, ·303-INCH RIFLE, No. 48, MARK I.

This **grenade** (Plate XLII) differs from the No. 42 Mark I (page 24) in containing four flash signals instead of a smoke candle, which are suspended from the parachute one below the other.

The signal stars consist of a rolled paper cylinder containing a perforated pellet of flash powder into which is inserted a paper tube filled with a charge of F.G. powder. The bottom of the star cylinder is closed with a perforated wood plug, into which is inserted a length of time fuze, a layer of priming mixture being coated over the exterior surface of the plug. The head of the cylinder is closed by a wood plug and covered by a calico cap.

The stars are attached to the parachute threads by asbestos cord which is tied round the caps at intervals of 2 feet. The intervening cord is coiled up and wrapped in white paper, the coils being packed into the space between the signals on assembly.

A descriptive label is attached to the tinned plate cap of the grenade.

GRENADE, ·303-INCH RIFLE, No. 51.

The **Marks I & II grenades** (*see* Plates XXXVII and XXXVIII) differ respectively from the No. 32 Marks II and III grenade (page 23) in being fitted with white illuminating stars instead of coloured stars.

They are similarly marked, but have in addition the words "Day or Night" stencilled lengthwise on the body alongside three white patches.

Lights, 26.

LIGHT, COASTGUARD.

The **Mark II light** (Plate XLIII) consists of a brown paper cylinder closed at the base by a layer of clay and a partly coned beechwood plug on to which a cone of X tin is secured by three iron nails. The cylinder is filled with six pellets of light composition and a layer of igniting composition is pressed in at the head, the light being closed by a paper cap which is provided with a stripping tape.

A small paper cylinder containing an igniter is secured to the light by a paper band pasted round the body.

The light is painted drab colour and has the words "Light, Coastguard II" stencilled on the side, and a paper label giving directions for lighting is pasted on.

LIGHTS, ILLUMINATING WRECKS.

The **Mark IV light** (Plate XLIV) consists of a cylindrical aluminium body made up in ten segments soldered together, each segment being filled with flare composition and primed at both ends with loose priming composition, a loose layer of the same composition being placed between each section.

The base of the body is closed with a wood block into which is fitted an iron wire hanging handle.

The head of the body is closed with a cap consisting of a millboard disc covered with osnaburg, having a stripping cord provided to facilitate removal. The osnaburg disc is dipped in Kit composition to prevent ingress of moisture.

The exterior of the body is painted red, with white bands round the joints of the sections.

The **Mark V light** (Plate XLV) differs from the Mark IV in the body being made in one piece instead of segments, and it is filled with flare composition to within $\frac{1}{4}$-inch of the mouth leaving a coned recess in the top for igniting mixture, and having a layer of mealed powder placed on the top. The cap is covered with dowlas instead of osnaburg and is similarly waterproofed.

The body is painted red.

LIGHT, LONG, RED.

The **Mark III light** (Plate XLVI) consists of a paper cylinder containing red light composition secured to a wood handle, a layer of clay being placed between the light composition and the wood handle. Igniting composition is placed on top of the light composition, and the cylinder closed by a paper cap which is provided with a calico stripping tape. A recess is bored in the wood handle and fitted with an igniter, which is a push-in fit.

The light is painted red, and has the words "Light, long, red, III" stencilled on the side, and a label showing nature, time of burning, and giving instructions for firing is pasted on.

LIGHT, LONG, GREEN.

The **Mark III light** (Plate XLVI) is made up similarly to the red light described above, differing only in the colour of the composition, and the body is painted green.

LIGHT, LONG, BLUE.

The **Mark III light** (Plate XLVI) is made up similarly to the red light described above, differing only in the colour of the composition, and the body is painted blue.

LIGHT, LONG, G.S.

The **Mark III light** (Plate XLVII) is made up in a similar manner to the light, long, red, Mark III, described on page 26 and is painted drab colour with the words "Light, long, G.S. III" stencilled in black on the side, a paper label giving directions for use being pasted on.

LIGHT, SHORT, G.S.

The **Mark II light** (Plate XLVIII) differs from the light, long, G.S. Mark III in having a shorter paper cylinder and consequently less light composition.

The light is painted drab colour with the words "Light, short, G.S. II" stencilled on the side, and has a direction label pasted on.

LIGHTS, V.B.S.

The **Mark I lights** (Plate XLIX), of which only a small number were made, consist of a cylindrical paper case with a brass base, cap chamber and cap, containing an aluminium cylinder holding two stars, either two red, two green, two white, or a red and green, the stars being separated by strands of quickmatch with a layer of call composition above and below the strands. A row of holes are made in the aluminium cylinder and quickmatch placed on the outside of the latter to communicate the flash from the propelling charge in the case to the quickmatch between the stars. The cartridges are closed by the mouth of the case being turned in over a cardboard or tinned or coppered sheet disc.

The cartridges are distinguished by two coloured bands round the mouth and have a white label on the closing disc bearing the word "Red" or "Green" or others as applicable. In addition, to facilitate identification in the dark, the cartridges have the rim treated as follows:—

When containing:—

2 red stars	rim of base milled all round.
2 green stars	rim left plain.
2 white stars	rim milled half round.
1 red and 1 green star	rim milled for the space of about $\frac{1}{4}$-inch in four equidistant places.

This marking, however, is being discontinued.

ROCKET, FLASH AND SOUND.

The **Mark I rocket** (Plate L) consists of a cylindrical brown paper body closed at the top with a perforated clay plug, filled with rocket composition primed at the bottom with mealed powder and closed by a screwed-in wood plug, the body being choked with twine at the rear end to form a vent for the rocket composition when ignited. A copper socket for the rocket stick is secured to the rear end with pack thread.

A cylindrical brown paper head is secured to the top of the body and contains 24 stars in six columns below a tin cylinder containing a flash explosive charge, the charge and stars being ignited by strands of quickmatch, leading to the rocket composition in the body.

The rocket is painted drab colour and has an instruction label pasted on the body.

ROCKET, LIFE-SAVING BOXER.

The **Mark VI rocket** (Plate LI) consists of a cylindrical body of solid drawn steel, in two sections, filled with rocket composition.

The two sections are connected by a wrought iron or mild steel connecting piece pinned into the bottom of the upper section and screwed into the mouth of the lower section. The head of the rocket is closed by a wood head, secured with iron tacks, a steel, lead and millboard disc being placed between the head and the rocket composition. A lead washer and millboard washer are placed between the connecting piece and the composition in the lower section of the body, and the latter is closed by a perforated mild steel base piece, the perforation being covered by a paper disc. A screwed recess is formed in the base piece to receive a metal plug for transit or storage purposes.

Clips for the reception of a 9-ft. 6-inch rocket stick are secured to the body, one at the head and the other at the tail.

The body of the rocket is painted red and instruction labels are pasted on the exterior.

METHOD OF FIRING.—The rocket stick and rope having been attached and the rocket placed in the machine, the metal closing plug is removed and the paper disc broken. A "Fuze, rocket, Boxer" is then placed into a cavity formed in the rocket composition and ignited by the flame of a "portfire."

The **Mark VI*** (Plate LII), which is an alternative pattern to the Mark VI, only differs from the latter in the tubes forming the body being drawn with solid lower ends, instead of having a separate connecting piece and base piece.

ROCKET, LIGHT, ½-LB.

The **Mark II rocket** (Plate LIII) consists of a cylindrical brown paper body closed at the base by a screwed wooden plug and at the top by a perforated plug of clay. A cylindrical brown paper head with conical cap is secured to the front of the body by a strip of white paper wound and pasted round the joint.

The head is filled with a magnesium star in a brown paper case and the body with rocket composition, a length of quickmatch passed through the central hole in the clay plug connecting the star and rocket composition. A conical recess is formed in the rocket composition which is primed at the mouth with powder and fitted with a length of safety fuze. The safety fuze is choked in position by pack thread wound round the body of the rocket and the free end is led through a hole in the side of the body and secured alongside the stick socket with twine. The copper socket for the stick is secured to the rear end of the body by pack thread and copper wire.

The body of the rocket is painted white and has an instruction label pasted on the side.

ROCKETS, LIGHT, PARACHUTE, RED,
ROCKETS, LIGHT, PARACHUTE, GREEN,
ROCKETS, LIGHT, PARACHUTE, WHITE.

The **Mark I rockets** (Plate LIV), which only differ from each other in the colour of the illuminating star, each consists of a cylindrical brown paper case containing rocket composition, with a paper head tapering out from the top and closed with a paper cone secured by a calico band. The bottom of the body is choked with twine over a length of safety fuze, the free end of which is passed through a hole in the side of the body and secured by a paper strip; a priming charge of mealed powder is placed in the body round the safety fuze and the body closed with a paper cap.

A friction ignition arrangement is affixed at the rear end of the rocket, stripping bands of tape being provided to bare the safety fuze and friction disc. Should the friction arrangement fail, the rocket may be ignited with a portfire. A socket is secured to the side for the reception of the rocket stick.

The head of the rocket contains a Japanese paper parachute attached to a red, white, or green illuminating star.

The point of the head is painted red or green when such stars are fitted, and the rest of the body drab; when a white star is fitted the rocket is painted drab all over.

An instruction label is pasted on the side.

ROCKET, LIGHT AND SOUND, 1-LB.

The **Mark I rocket** (Plate LV) is made up similarly to the rocket, light, ½-lb. (page 30) except that the head is closed by a wood plug, bayonet jointed, and contains a tonite charge and illuminating star. The lower end of the tonite charge has a central recess formed in it to take a copper detonator, and it is separated from the star by a perforated felt wad.

The head of the rocket is painted red and the body drab, and an instruction label is pasted on the side.

ROCKET, ANTI-ZEPPELIN, BROCK'S.

The **Mark I rocket** (Plate LVI) consists of a cylindrical case of millboard with a pyramidal steel nose screwed on to one end, and choked near the opposite end round which is wound the binding for securing a copper socket for a 5-ft. wood stick.

A ¾-inch layer of clay is placed under the nose below which is a 1¼-inch layer of grey composition, the remainder of the body being filled with black rocket composition in which is left a conical recess.

The rocket is fired by means of an electric primer inserted at the choked end.

ROCKET, MESSAGE CARRYING.

The **Mark I rocket** (Plate LVII) is composed of the following principal parts:—Body with collar and closing discs, spigot with locking spring and pin, rear or tail tube with vanes, message holder, whistle and range flanges.

The body consists of a steel tube 1·3775-inch internal diameter, spun over at the head and closed with a mild steel closing disc, and is fitted at the rear end with a mild steel spigot secured by six dowel pins held in position by the steel collar, which is in turn secured by two screws passing through the collar and body into the spigot.

The steel spigot is recessed at the head, and has three oblique channels cut equidistantly round the edge to act as escapes. Below the head the spigot is slightly tapered and is bored out to receive the rear or tail tube. The tail tube is retained in position by the locking spring and pin, the spring being screwed to the exterior of the spigot in such a position that the pin engages in corresponding holes drilled in the wall of both the spigot and tail tube.

The tail portion consists of a seamless steel tube divided internally into two compartments by a diaphragm composed of a wood plug and tin discs. Three tinned iron vanes are soldered to the exterior near the rear end in a slightly oblique position, which has the dual effect of steadying the rocket and causing it to rotate during flight.

The body of the rocket is filled with rocket composition, in which a recess is formed for the reception of a length of quickmatch connected to a "Brock's" igniter, secured into one of the oblique slots in the head of the spigot.

The front chamber of the tail tube contains a twisted iron wire message holder, and the rear chamber is filled with layers of smoke composition, flare composition, delay composition between two layers of priming composition, the end of the tube being closed by dipping in match composition.

The whistle is made of brass and is pressed over the head of the rocket.

The three brass flanges, which only differ from each other in width of lip, are shaped to fit the head of the whistle and are for adjusting the range of flight as follows:—

    1st flange (small lip) for range of 1,600 yards.
    2nd ,, (medium lip)   ,,   1,300 ,,
    3rd ,, (large lip)   ,,   850 ,,

The tail portion of the rocket is fitted with a cylindrical strawboard protecting cylinder, over which is placed a waterproofed calico cover, the body also being fitted with a similar cover. The mouth of each cover is secured round the tail portion by insulated tape bindings.

Instructions for firing, on printed labels, are pasted round the rocket, and a caution label as to the removal of protecting covering is gummed on to the exterior of the head cover.

ROCKET, AERODROME FLARE.

The **Mark I aerodrome flare rocket** (Plate LVIII) is made up similarly to the message carrying rocket (page 31) except that the message holder and the charge of smoke composition in the tail tube are omitted; the tail tube is made in two parts and secured to the body of the rocket by a screwed stud instead of by a spring clip.

The head of the rocket is fitted with a brass nose piece, and the whistle and range flanges are omitted.

ROCKET, SIGNAL, 1½-INCH, PISTOL.

The **Mark I rocket** (Plate LIX) consists of a cylindrical case of brown paper, partly choked with string near the base, and closed with a wood plug in the base, and a pyramidal nose of wood at the top.

Three triangular sticks, with tops bound with tape, are secured to the case with three rows of binding, a paper collar glued to the case near the centre keeping them at an angle in order to leave the bottom of the case clear for inserting in the pistol.

The inside of the case below the choke is coated with priming composition to convey the flash to the black composition in the body.

The base plug is bored to receive a piece of Bickford fuze and charge of black powder, which communicates the flash to the priming composition.

ROCKET, SIGNAL, 1-lb. SERVICE.

The **Mark III rocket** (Plate LX) consists of a cylindrical brown paper body, closed at the top with a perforated clay plug, filled with rocket composition, primed at the bottom with powder and closed by a screwed-in wood plug. The body is choked with twine near the base, and is fitted with a socket for the rocket stick.

A cylindrical brown paper head with conical paper cap is secured to the body and contains 28 white stars in four columns and some mealed powder which serves to open the star case and scatter the stars.

The exterior of the rocket is painted white and has an instructional label pasted on the side.

ROCKETS, SIGNAL, 1-lb., RED.
ROCKETS, SIGNAL, 1-lb., BLUE.
ROCKETS, SIGNAL, 1-lb., GREEN.

The **Mark II rocket** (Plate LXI), which only differ from each other in the colour of the stars contained, are similar to the 1-lb. Service Rocket described above except that they have a larger head with rounded cap, filled with 49 coloured stars in seven columns, and are packed in with quickmatch which ignites them and opens the head.

The head of the rocket is painted red, blue, or green according to the colour of the stars contained, and the body painted drab colour; an instruction label is pasted round the side.

Rockets, 34.

ROCKET, SIGNAL, 1-lb., RED AND WHITE.

The **Mark II rocket** (Plate LXII) is made up similarly to the 1-lb. red rocket described on page 33 differing in containing 25 red and white stars, and in the stick socket which is made of paper instead of copper, affixed near the top of the body. A puff of powder is placed in the top of the socket and communicates by means of a flash hole and quickmatch with the composition in the body, the object being to explode the socket and separate the stick from the case.

The exterior of the rocket is painted drab colour with longitudinal red stripes painted round the head, and an instruction label is pasted on the side.

ROCKET, SIGNAL, 1-lb.

Magnesium, "Meteor."

The **rockets** (Plate LXIII) consist of a cylindrical brown paper body closed at the base by a screwed wooden plug and at the top by a perforated plug of clay. A cylindrical brown paper head with conical cap of wood or paper is glued to the top of the body and secured by a strip of white paper wound and pasted round the joint. The body is choked near the lower end and bound with pack thread.

The head is filled with a red or white magnesium star in an aluminium case, and the body with rocket composition, a length of quickmatch passing through the hole in the clay plug connecting the star with the rocket composition. A conical recess is formed in the rocket composition which is primed at the mouth with powder and fitted with a length of safety fuze led through a hole in the side and secured to a friction board glued to the body and covered with a tear-off strip of tape.

A socket of tinned sheet iron for the stick is secured to the lower part of the body with pack thread, and a paper cylinder to receive an igniter plug which is primed with amorphous phosphorus is glued to the centre of the body and secured by a linen strip glued on.

The body is painted grey and the head red when a red star is enclosed, the whole rocket being painted grey when it contains a white star.

A label giving the designation of the rocket and the colour of the star, with instructions for fixing the stick, is pasted on the body.

ACTION.—The stick having been secured, the wood plug and tear-off strip removed, the igniter plug is rubbed over the patch of friction composition firing the fuze which burns for about five seconds and ignites the priming in the mouth of the rocket

The rocket rises to a height of 600 feet, the star burning for about ten seconds.

ROCKET, SIGNAL, ½-lb. SERVICE.

The **Mark III rocket** (Plate LXIV) resembles the 1-lb. Service Rocket (page 33) except in size and in the star case being slightly larger in diameter than the body and containing only 20 stars in five columns.

It is painted white and has an instruction label pasted on the side.

ROCKETS, SIGNAL, ½-lb., RED, MARK II.
ROCKETS, SIGNAL, ½-lb., BLUE, MARK II.
ROCKETS, SIGNAL, ½-lb., GREEN, MARK II.

These **rockets** (Plate LXV) are made up and painted similarly to the 1-lb. rockets (page 33) but are of course smaller and the head contains 30 stars in five columns.

ROCKETS, SOUND, ½-lb.

The **Mark II rocket** (Plate LXVI) has the body made up similarly to the ½-lb. light rocket (page 30) but the head, which is larger in diameter, has a 2-oz. pellet of guncotton instead of a star, the guncotton being detonated by a fulminate detonator contained in the centre and connected with the rocket composition in the body by quickmatch. The top of the head is closed by a calico bag tied with tape.

The **Mark III rocket** (Plate LXVII) differs from the Mark II in having a tonite charge instead of guncotton, and in the detonator being slightly different.

The head is closed by a wood plug secured by means of a bayonet joint, and the base of the rocket is closed with a paper covering instead of a screwed-in wood plug.

The **Mark II rocket** is painted drab colour and the **Mark III** is painted black, each rocket having an instruction label pasted on the side.

ROCKETS, WAR.

The **24-pr. Mark VII rocket** (Plate LXVIII) consists of a cylindrical steel body closed at the top with a cast-iron wood-lined head secured by 10 screws. It is filled with rocket composition and closed at the base with a wrought-iron base piece which is bored out, recessed and screwed to receive a tail piece and safety cap.

The tail piece is made of cast iron and has three tapering vents formed in it, the large end of the taper being toward the interior. The vents are cut away on one side in order that the gas issuing from them, when in flight, shall give the rocket a rotary movement, thus steadying the flight and preventing the rocket "tumbling."

The safety cap is made of mild steel in the shape of a dome and is removed before the rocket is fired.

The rocket is fired by means of a "Tube, friction, quill, long" in Naval Service, and "Tube, friction, copper, short" in Land Service.

The body is painted red and has a label pasted on giving instructions for firing.

The **9-pr. Mark VII rocket** (Plate LXIX) is similar in construction to the 24-pr. rocket, and is similarly painted.

SIGNALS, MORTAR, PARACHUTE, DAYLIGHT.
RED, BLUE, YELLOW, AND PURPLE.

The **Mark I signals** (Plate LXX) which differ from each other only in the colour of the smoke star, consist of a cylindrical brown paper body closed at the top with either a coned wooden head or cardboard disc secured by an adhesive calico band, and at the bottom with a wood plug. A rice-paper parachute and smoke star are assembled under the head, the two being connected by an asbestos cord; below the star is placed a perforated felt wad and through which are passed strands of quickmatch leading from holes in the star, and passing underneath the wad on to a primed calico disc. The space between the calico disc and the inner surface of the base plug is filled with a bursting charge of one dram of F.G. powder.

A paper fuze case containing quickmatch and ignitary mixture fits into a central perforation in the bottom plug.

The rear of the body is fitted with a paper case filled with a 1-oz. F.G. powder propelling charge, the mouth of the case being drawn in and choked with string.

A length of instantaneous fuze is led from the propelling charge case, laid up alongside the body and secured near the top by binding with twine. The top of the instantaneous fuze is splayed out and grafted on to a short length of Bickford fuze which is fitted with a lead foil cap.

The signal is painted drab colour with a coloured sinuous mark painted on the side to denote colour of smoke star contained and the star case also has a similar sinuous mark painted on.

A label giving instructions for use and designation of signal is pasted round the body.

SIGNAL, MORTAR, PARACHUTE, NIGHT.

The **Mark I signal** (Plate LXXI) is similar in construction to the daylight signal described above, differing in being fitted with three illuminating stars in combinations of red, green, yellow, and white.

The body of the signal is painted drab, and has three coloured discs painted on the side to denote colour of the illuminating star contained, and a similar disc is painted on the case of each star.

A paper label giving designation of signal and instructions for firing is pasted on the body.

The **Mark II signal** (Plate LXXII) differs from the Mark I in having a slightly larger case, the wood top of which is extended into a neck through which a short length of safety fuze is led, the top being coated with priming powder and covered with a tin cap secured with a tear-off tape.

Signals, 38.

The base is closed by a flat wood block hollowed out to take the propelling charge, which is kept in place by a cardboard disc. The upper portion of the wood block is drilled to take the fuze connecting with the opening charge, which in turn ignites the stars by means of communicating quickmatch. The stars are slightly different in construction. The safety fuze in the head is connected with the propelling charge by means of quickmatch which passes down a groove in the outside of the case and under the cardboard disc.

The parachute is slightly smaller and is not made up in sections as in the Mark I.

The signal is painted, marked, and has an instruction label similarly to the Mark I.

SIGNALS, SOCKET, LIGHT, AND SOUND.
GREEN, RED, AND WHITE.

The **Mark I signals** (Plate LXXIII) consist of a cylindrical body of tinned steel, lap jointed, head of wood with rubber cap, base of cast iron with steel cap, two fuze tubes, central tube of brass and rubber, bag for propelling charge. The upper part of the body contains either four green, five red or three white star rings, the lower one having a priming ring of gunpowder, and the lower part contains the sound detonating charge of 4 oz. of tonite with two time fuzes and detonator. The bag, containing the propelling charge of $2\frac{1}{2}$ oz. of blasting powder, is secured to the base by rubber solution. The central tube is fitted with an igniter consisting of a brass tube containing, in the order named, an anvil, percussion cap, striker, spiral spring, and brass tube distance piece. The top end is closed by a brass plug with a central hole through which a copper wire attached to the striker is passed, the wire being twisted into a loop on the outside.

ACTION.—On pulling the wire of the igniter, the spring is compressed, and on release the striker moves downwards and fires the cap which in turn fires the propelling charge in the base of the signal.

The body of the signal is painted with aluminium paint.

Index, 39.

INDEX TO CONTENTS.

Para. L. of C.	Designation.	Service.	Detail.	Design Number.	Page.	Plate.
	Bombs, 3·45-inch—		electric ignition.			
	Signal flare, red—					
18737	Mark I	A.		C.I.W. 2354		I
19306	Mark II	A.		I.D.W. 291 2		II
18146 / 18821	Signal flare, white, Mark I‡	A.		R.L. 22446A(1)		III
18146 / 21505	Signal, smoke— Mark I†	A.		R.L. 22035B(1)		IV
18822	Mark II	A.		R.L. 24078A		—
21054	Mark III‡	A.		R.L. 24078B		V
	Parachute, flare— Mark I†	A.		R.L. 22749		—
18146 21322 21323 22620 23232	Mark II†	A.		R.L. 22749		—
	Mark III†	A.		R.L. 22749A		—
	Mark IV†	A.		R.L. 22749c		—
	Mark V†	A.		R.L. 22749D		VI
21324	Reconnaissance flare—					
21663	9 seconds delay, Mark I	A.		R.L. 27639		VII
	Bomb, triple flare—					
20637 20640 22543 23133	12 secs. delay 6 secs. delay 2½ secs. delay } Mk. I‡	A.	("Holt Pattern") with parachute.	I.D.W. B/70		VIII
	Bomb, 4·2-inch signal— Coloured smoke, Mark I‡	A.	with striker	{ T.W.D. 6013 T.W.D. 6014		IX
	Bomb, 4·5-inch signal—					
21652	Smoke, Mark I‡	A.	(Pain's No. 3); with friction igniter	I.D.W. 2921		X

† Obsolete for future manufacture.
‡ Obsolete.

Index, 40.

Para. L. of C.	Designation	Service	Detail	Design Number	Plate
21943	**Bomb, ground flare—** Mark I...	A.		T.W.D. 6177 6178 6179	XI
22955	**Bomb, message carrying, aerial—** Mark I...	A.	with striker releasing lever (Geake pattern).	T.W.D. 6367	XII
	Candle, smoke, ground—				
19244 } 22959 }	Mark I‡	L.	type "S"	I.D.W. 4028	} XIII
19774	Mark II	L.	type "S.1."	I.D.W. 4069	
	Cartridges, illuminating— 1½-inch parachute—				
17361 } 23383 }	Mark I‡	L.	...	C.I.W. 1973	XIV
21965 } 23383 }	Mark II‡ Mark III	L. A.	...	I.D.W. 3859	} XV
	1½-inch dark ignition—				
17361 } 23383 }	Mark I‡	L.A.	...	C.I.W. 1974	} XVI
21965 } 23383 }	Mark II	A.	...	I.D.W. 3859	
	1-inch—				
17361 18839	Mark I Mark II	L. L.	} dark ignition	I.D.W. 3860	XVII
	Cartridges, signal, 1½-inch— White—				
22198 } 23383 }	Mark I‡	A.	for use from aircraft	C.I.W. 2325	} XVIII
	Mark II	A.	for use from aircraft	I.D.W. 3859	
	Red Green Yellow } without smoke, Mark I	A.	...	I.D.W. 3859	XIX
22198 23383	Red Green } with smoke, Mark I	A.	} for use from aircraft	I.D.W. 3859	XX
	Red Green } with smoke, Mark II	A.			XXI

‡ Obsolete.

Index, 41.

Para. L. of O.	Designation.	Service.	Detail.	Design Number.	Page.	Plate.
	Cartridges, signal, 1½-inch—*cont.*					
	Parachute, changing white to—					
22198	Rod, Mk. I	A.		I.D.W. 8859		XXII
23383	Green, Mk. 1	A.				
	With parachute and coloured smoke—					
	Mark I	A.	for use from aircraft	I.D.W. 4191		XXIII
23313	Mark II	A.	for use from aircraft	I.D.W. 4524		XXIV
22198	With changing colour star,					
23383	Mark I	A.	for use from aircraft	I.D.W. 4511		XXV
	Three star, dark ignition—					
22887	Mark I	A.		I.D.W. 4554		XXVI
	Mark II	A.				
	Parachute, reduced charge,					
23314	Mark I	A.		I.D.W. 8859		See Plate XV
	With scintillating star—					
22631	Mark I‡	L.		I.D.W. 4578		XXVII
23383	Mark II‡	L.				
	Cartridges, signal, 1-inch—					
	Aircraft, white—					
17563	Mark I	A.	for use from aircraft	I.D.W. 8860		XXVIII
17551	Mark II	A.				
	Black streamer—					
18853	Mark I†	N.		I.D.W. 8860		XXIX
23250	Mark II†	N.				
	Green—					
17363	Mark IV	C.A.		I D.W. 3860 for N.S.		
17551	Mark V	C.A.				
	Red—					
22199	Mark IV	C.A.		I.D.W. 4574 for L.S. & A.S.		XXX
22632	Mark V	C.A				
23232	White—					
	Mark IV	C.A.				
	Mark V	C.A.				
	Yellow—					
22632	Mark IV	L A.		I.D.W. 4574		
23232	Mark V	L.A.				
18677	**Flare, ground, ½-hour,** red, Mark I	L.		I.D.W. 4004		XXXI

† Obsolete for future manufacture.
‡ Obsolete.

Index, 42.

Para. L. of C.	Designation.	Service.	Detail.	Design Number.	Page.	Plate.
19458	**Flares, ground—** 3-inches long by 2-inches diam.— Red, Green, Yellow, White } Mk. I	L.	...	I.D.W. 3866		XXXII
19458 {	**Flares, ground—** 1¾-inches long by 2 inches diameter— Red, Green, Yellow, White } Mk. I	L.	...	I.D.W. 3866		} XXXII
	1½ inches long by 1½ inches diameter— Red, Green, Yellow, White } Mk. I	L.	...	I.D.W. 3866		
17428 {	**Flares, signal—** Red, Mark I Green, Mark I	N. N.	} for Lloyds signal stations	I.D.W. 2160		XXXIII
23044 {	**Flares, landing—** 1 minute— Red tint, Mk. I§ Deep red, Mk. I§ 2 minute— Red tint, Mk. I Deep red, Mk. I	A. A. A. A.	... ...	} I.D.W. 4559		XXXIV
	Grenades, ·303-inch rifle—					
20469	No. 31, daylight signal— Mark I†‡	C.	tinned plate; cylindrical with dished ends, with parachute and smoke candle	I.D.W. 4019 4058		
· 20469	Mark II†	C.	tinned plate; cylindrical with dished base, with parachute and smoke candle	I.D.W. 4019 4198		XXXV
	Mark III†	C.				XXXVI*

† Obsolete for future manufacture.
‡ Only a small number made, none of which were issued to the Service.
§ Obsolete.

Index, 43.

Para. L. of C.	Designation.	Service.	Detail.	Design Number.	Page.	Plate.
	Grenades, ·303-inch rifle-*contd.* No. 32, night signal—					
20469	Mark I†‡	C.	tinned plate; cylindrical with dished ends, with parachute and stars	I.D.W. 4019 4060		—
20469	Mark II†	C.	tinned plate; cylindrical with dished base, with parachute and coloured stars	I.D.W. 4184 4019		XXXVII
21060 21061	Mark III†	C.				XXXVIII
21062	No. 38, night signal, Mark II†§	L.	tinned plate; cylindrical with dished base; with parachute and changing colour star	I.D.W. 4163		XXXIX
22191	No. 42, day signal, Mark 1	L.	paper body, cylindrical; with parachute, and smoke candle; for use with grenade discharger	T.W.D. 6234		XL
22190	No. 45, night signal, Mark I	L.	paper body, cylindrical; with parachute and changing colour star; for use with grenade discharger	T.W.D. 6235		XLI
22965	No. 48, day or night locality signal, Mark 1	L.	paper body; cylindrical; with parachute and four flash signals; for use with grenade discharger	T.W.D. 6530		XLII
4	No. 51, day or night signal— Mark I†	L.	tinned plate, cylindrical; with dished base; with parachute and white illuminating stars	I.D.W. 4184 4019 4060		*See* Plates XXXVII XXXVIII
	Mark II†	L.				

† Obsolete for future manufacture.
‡ Only a small number made, none of which were issued to the Service.
§ No Mark I grenades issued to the Service.

Index, 44.

Para L. of C.	Designation.	Service.	Detail.	Design Number.	Page.	Plate.
	Lights—					
6911	Coastguard, Mark II	N.		R.L. 7295		XLIII
4009	Illuminating wrecks, Mark IV	O.		R.L. 2464		XLIV
16540	Mark V†	L.		R.L. 17022		XLV
11880 13604 23390	Long, red, Mark III‖	C.		C.I.W. 711		
11830 23390	Long, green, Mark III‖	C.		C.I.W. 710		XLVI
11830	Long, blue, Mark III	N.		C.I.W. 708		
11830 23390	Long, G.S., Mark III‖	C.		C.I.W. 706		XLVII
11830 23390 21519	Short, G.S., Mark II‖	O.		O.I.W. 707		XLVIII
	V.B.S., Mark I‡	N.		I.D.W. 4037		XLIX
	Rockets—					
16541 17255	Flash and sound 1-lb. Mark I†	N.		O.I.W. 1729		L
10354	Life saving, boxer— Mark VI	L.		R.L. 11103		LI
14281	Mark VI*	L.		R.L. 14748(1)		LII
4652 23390	Light, ½-lb., Mark II§	L.		R.L. 4460		LIII
19252 23390	Light, parachute— Red, Mark I§ Green, Mark I§ White, Mark I§	L. L. L.		I.D.W. 3052		LIV
11448 14751 23232 23390	Light and sound, 1-lb., Mark I‖	C.	combined	C.I.W. 665		LV
18855 22474	Anti-Zeppelin, Brocks, Mark I§	N.		I.D.W. 3867		LVI
21521 22629	Message carrying, Mark I	L.	with tail tube and message holder	T.W.D. 5726 5798		LVII
22629	Aerodrome flare, Mark I	A.		T.W.D. 6397 R.L. 28718		LVIII

† Obsolete.
‡ Only a small number made.
§ Obsolete for future manufacture.
‖ Obsolete for future manufacture. L.S. only.

Index, 45.

Para. L. of C.	Designation.	Service.	Detail.	Design Number.	Page.	Plate.
	Rockets—*contd.*					
20639	Signal, 1½-inch, pistol, Mark I‡	N.		I.D.W. 4012		LIX
17255, 23390	Signal, 1-lb., service, Mark III§	C.		R.L. 4457		LX
4572, 13164, 23390	Signal, 1-lb. red, Mark II§	C.				
	Signal, 1-1b., blue, Mark II§	O.		R.L. 4455		LXI
	Signal, 1-1b., green, Mark II§	C.				
4572, 13605, 23390	Signal, 1-lb., red and white — Mark II‡	L		R.L. 4456		LXII
22280, 23390	Signal, 1-lb., magnesium, "Meteor"— Red, Mark I§ White, Mark I§	L.A. L.A.		T.W.D. 6132		LXIII
4572, 13161, 23390	Signal, ½-lb., service, Mark III‡	L.		RL/4459		LXIV
	Signal, ½-lb., red, Mark II‡	L.				
	Signal, ½-1b., blue, Mark II‡	L.		R.L. 4458		LXV
	Signal, ½-lb., green, Mark II‡	L.				
4652, 14751, 23390	Sound, ½-lb.— Mark II§	O.		R.L. 4461		LXVI
11066, 14751, 23990	Mark III§	C.		C.I.W. 644		LXVII
4760, 22864	War, 24-pr., Mark VII†	C.	with steel safety cap	R.L. 4524		LXVIII
5111, 22864	War, 9-pr., Mark VII†	C.		R.L. 5282		LXIX
	Signal, mortar, parachute— Daylight—					
18968, 22196, 22885	Red, Blue, Yellow, Purple } Mk. I†	L.	with smoke candle	I.D.W. 4003		LXX
18968, 20296, 22885	Night— Mark I†	L.	with stars	I.D.W. 4005		LXXI
	Mark II†	L.		I.D.W. 4067		LXXII
	Signal, socket, light and sound—					
19942	Green, Mark I	L.				
19942, 20610	Red, Mark I	O.		I.D.W. 2109		LXXIII
20909	White, Mark I	L.				

† Obsolete.
‡ Obsolete for future manufacture.
§ Obsolete for future manufacture. L.S. only.

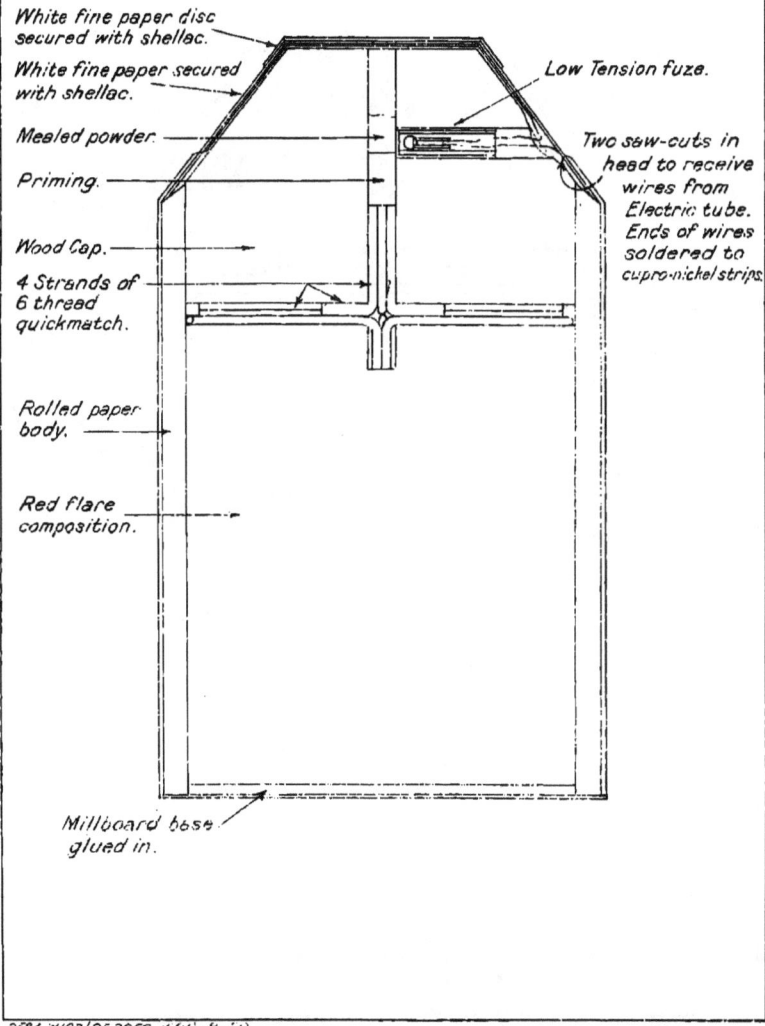

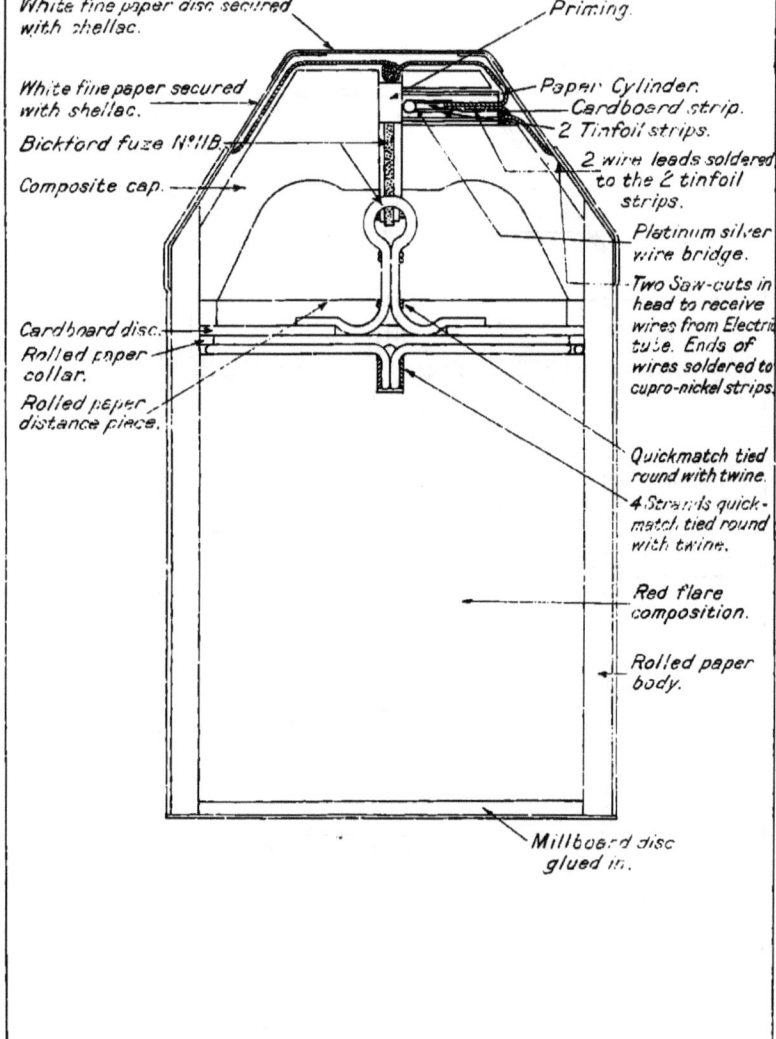

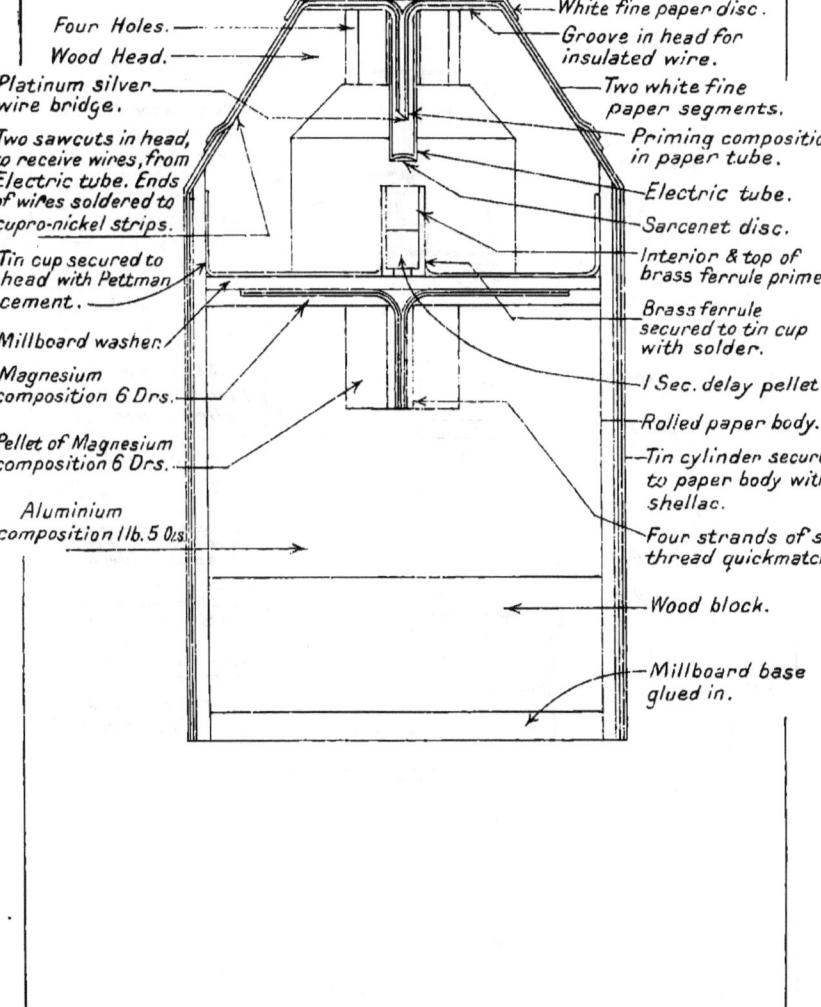

Plate III.

BOMB, 3·45 INCH, SIGNAL, FLARE, WHITE (MK.I.) ELECTRIC IGNITION.

Plate IV.

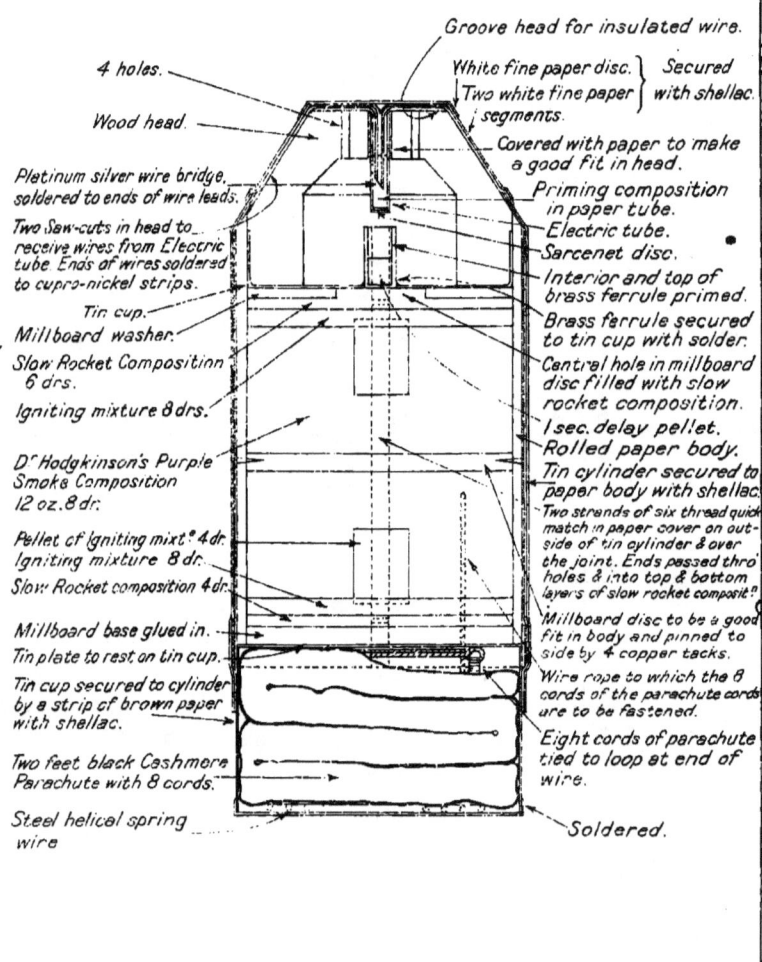

Plate V.

BOMB, 3·45 INCH, SIGNAL, SMOKE, MARK III.
ELECTRIC IGNITION.

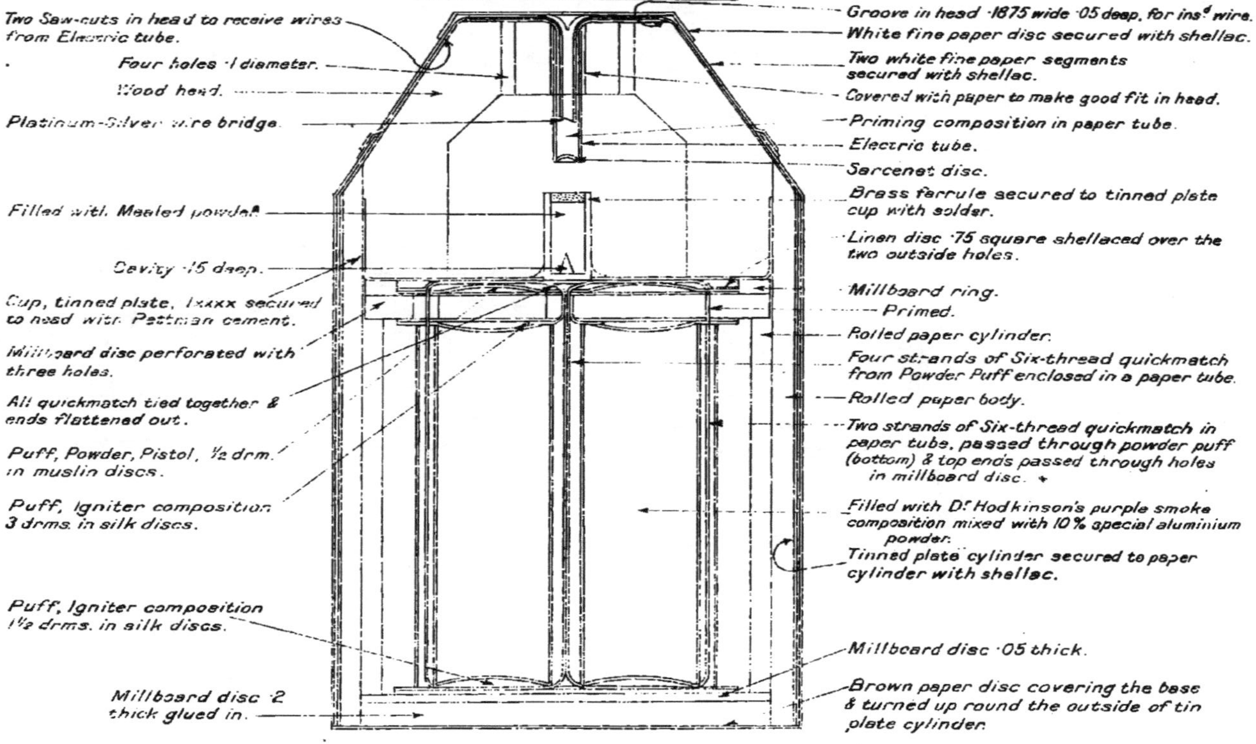
Two Saw-cuts in head to receive wires from Electric tube.
Four holes ·1 diameter.
Wood head.
Platinum-Silver wire bridge.
Filled with Mealed powder.
Cavity ·15 deep.
Cup, tinned plate, Ixxxx secured to head with Pettman cement.
Millboard disc perforated with three holes.
All quickmatch tied together & ends flattened out.
Puff, Powder, Pistol, ½ drm. in muslin discs.
Puff, Igniter composition 3 drms. in silk discs.
Puff, Igniter composition 1½ drms. in silk discs.
Millboard disc ·2 thick glued in.
Groove in head ·1875 wide ·05 deep, for insd wire.
White fine paper disc secured with shellac.
Two white fine paper segments secured with shellac.
Covered with paper to make good fit in head.
Priming composition in paper tube.
Electric tube.
Sarcenet disc.
Brass ferrule secured to tinned plate cup with solder.
Linen disc ·75 square shellaced over the two outside holes.
Millboard ring.
Primed.
Rolled paper cylinder.
Four strands of Six-thread quickmatch from Powder Puff enclosed in a paper tube.
Rolled paper body.
Two strands of Six-thread quickmatch in paper tube, passed through powder puff (bottom) & top ends passed through holes in millboard disc.
Filled with Dr Hodkinson's purple smoke composition mixed with 10% special aluminium powder.
Tinned plate cylinder secured to paper cylinder with shellac.
Millboard disc ·05 thick.
Brown paper disc covering the base & turned up round the outside of tin plate cylinder.

9584. W150/PP3656.
Malby & Sons, Lith.

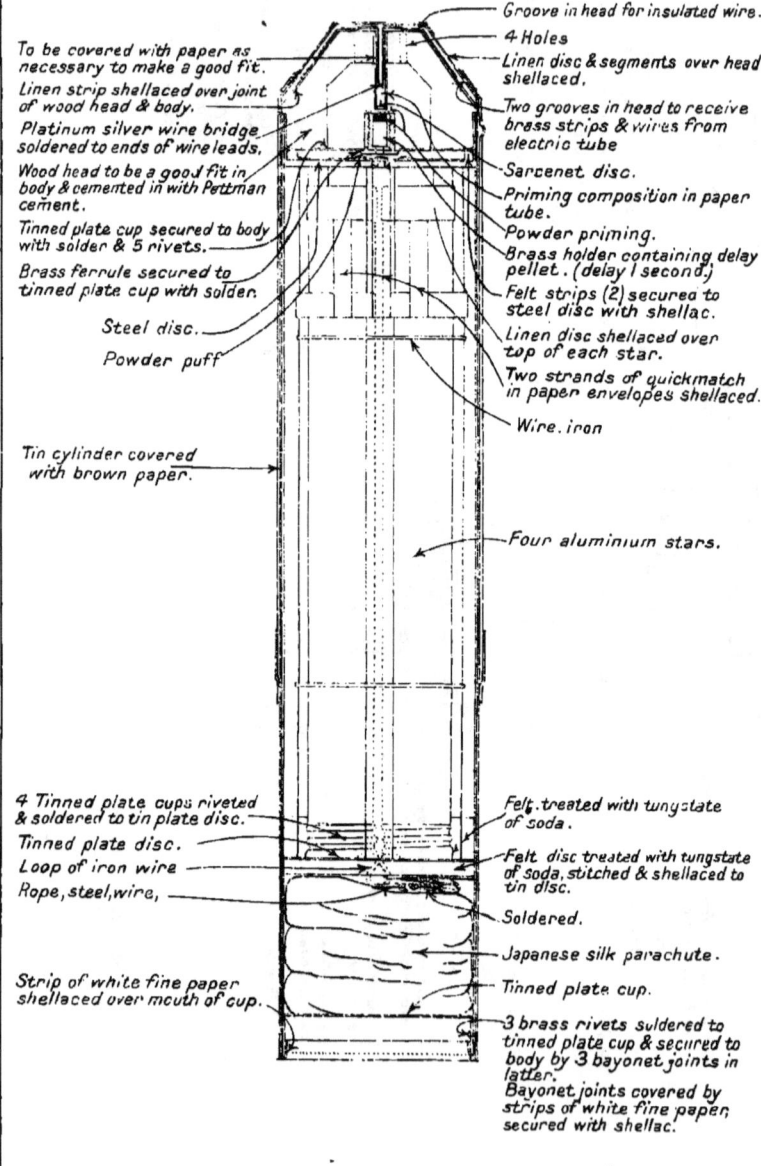

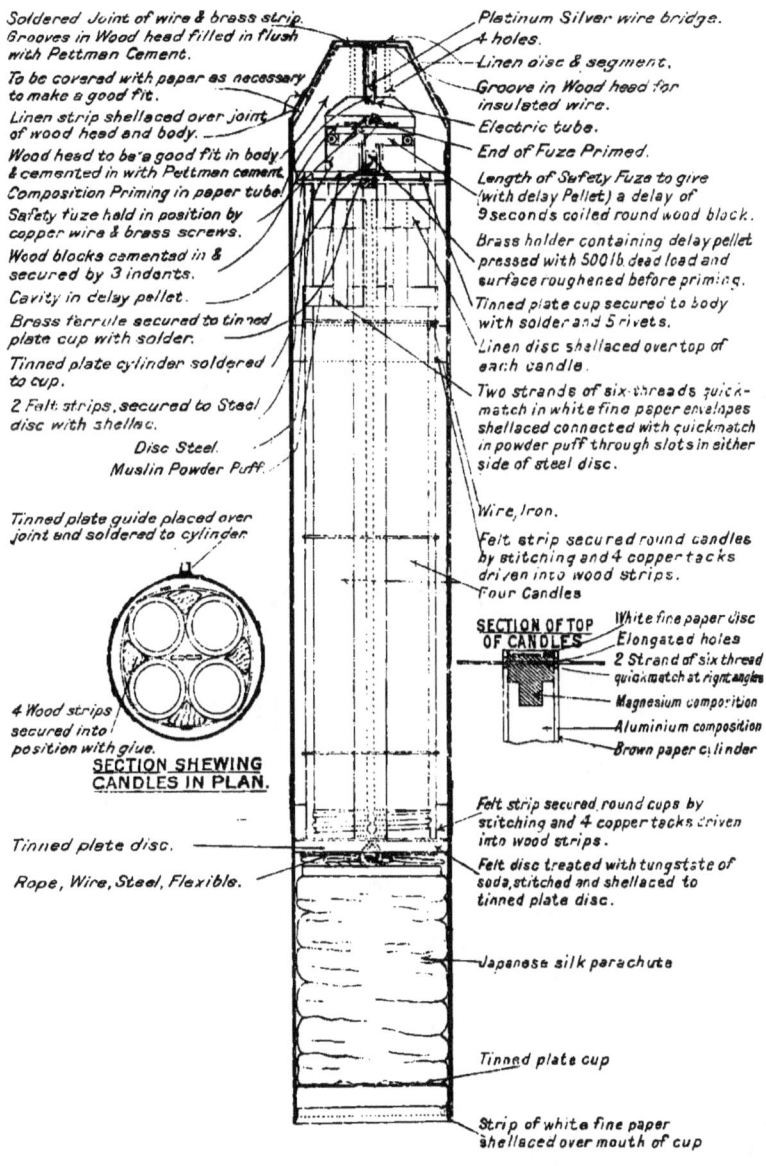

Plate VIII.

BOMB, TRIPLE FLARE, MARK I.

12 SECONDS DELAY	A	
6 SECONDS DELAY	A	("HOLT PATTERN") WITH PARACHUTE.
2½ SECONDS DELAY	A	

Friction fuze.
Brown paper cylinder.
Paper covering.
Calico covering.
Brown paper cylinder.
Quickmatch.
Marine glue.
Calico covering.
Igniting composition.
Brown paper cylinder.
Aluminium composition.
Calico covering.
Calico band 1·0 wide.
1 Oz. of shot.
Clay.
Brown paper disc.
Marine glue.
String

Two turns of twine.
Body to be coated with Aluminium paint.
Calico strip.
Safety fuze, one length to each candle.
Two turns of twine.
Two turns of twine.

9584

Maltby & Sons, Lith.

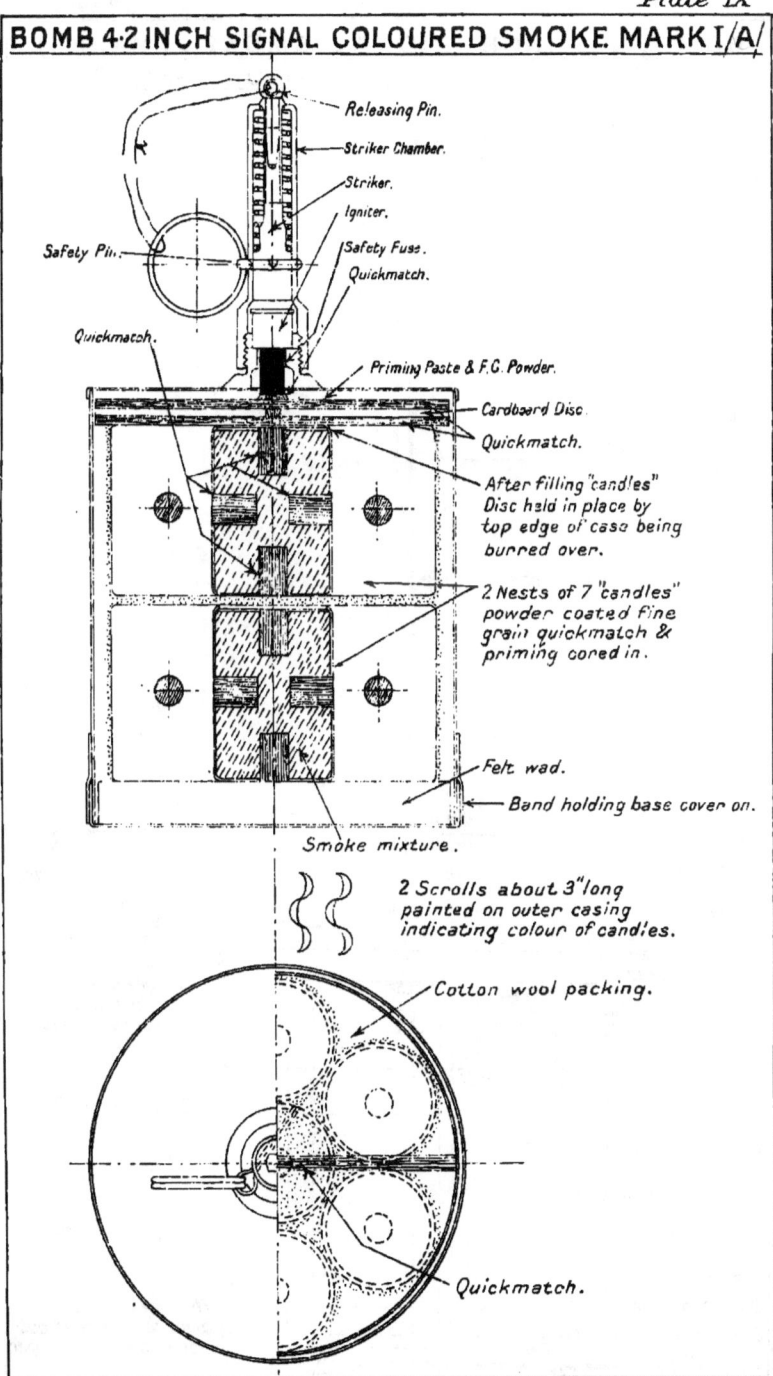

Plate X

BOMB, 4·5 INCH, SIGNAL SMOKE. (MARK I).
(PAINS Nº 3) WITH FRICTION IGNITER.

- Quickmatch coated with igniting composition
- Paper Case
- Paper case coated with igniting composition
- Quickmatch in calico case
- Held by a rubber band during transit.
- Fuze Case
- 5 of firework fuze
- 2 Strawboard discs secured to Body and Fuze case with glue.
- 4 strands of quickmatch tied together with twine.
- Paper bag filled with 2oz. of coarse grain black powder the top primed outside with mealed powder
- Clay
- Rubber Band
- Rolled paper case
- Smoke composition
- Paper Case.
- Clay
- Strawboard Disc
- Calico secured round body and to bottom disc.
- The body top & bottom discs to be covered outside with white fine paper.

9584

Malby & Sons Lith

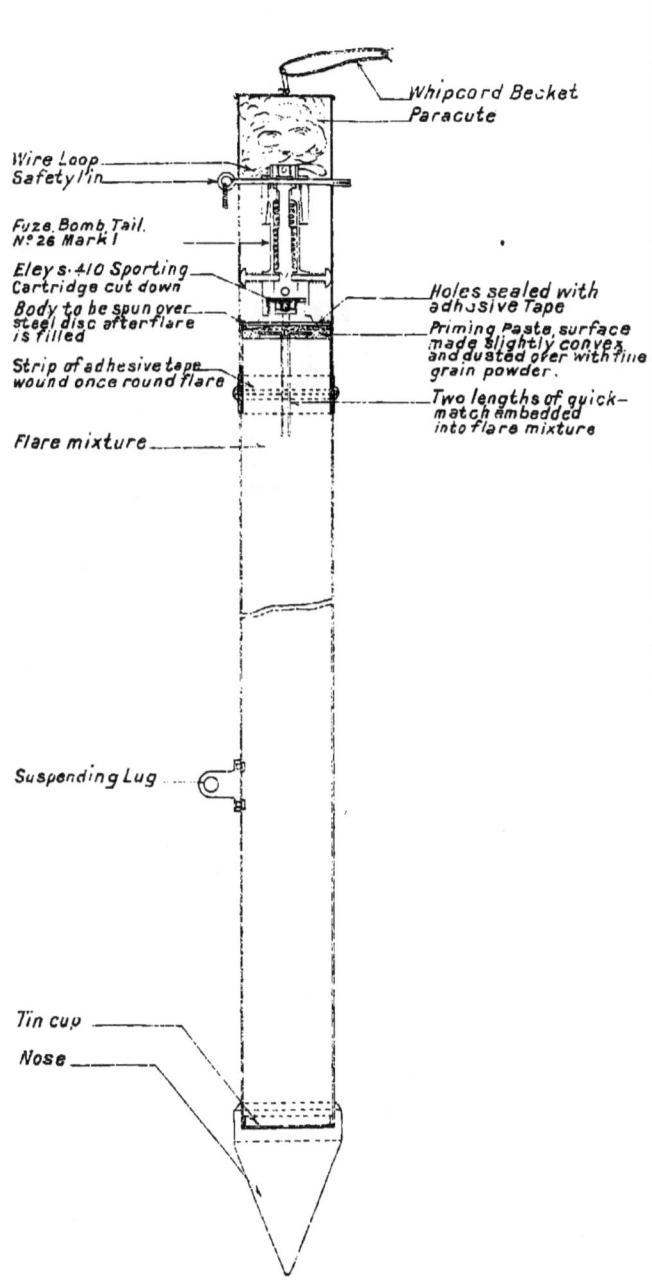

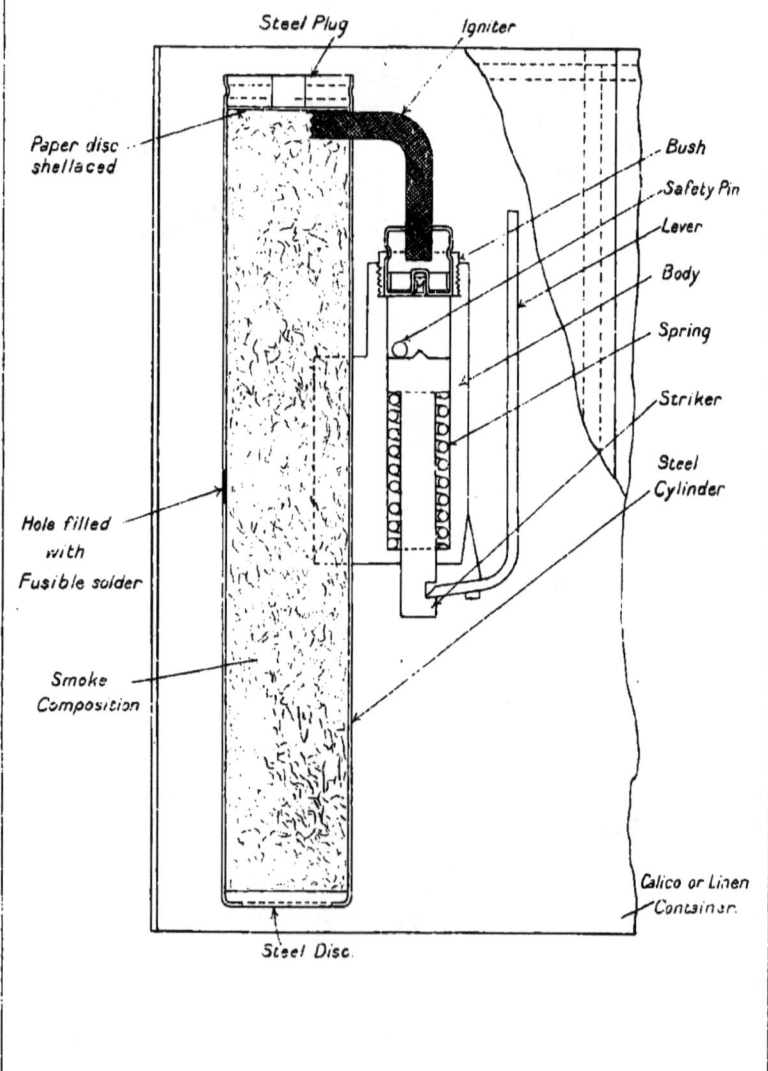

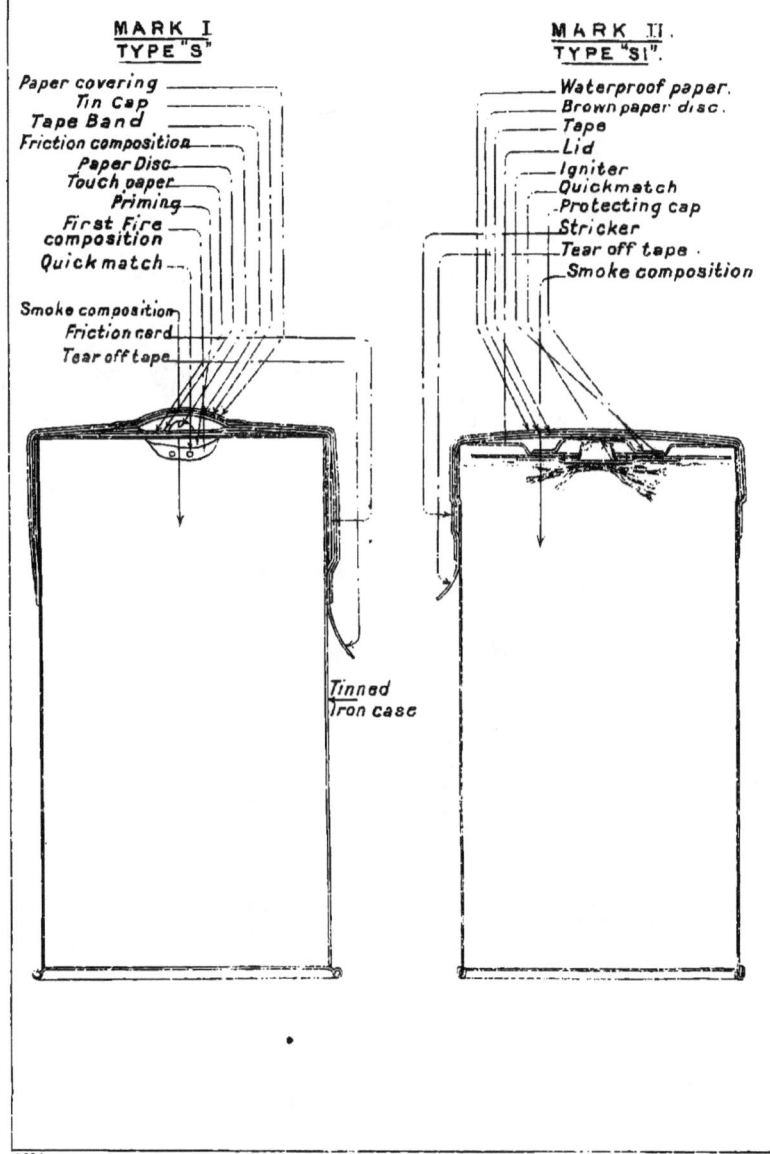

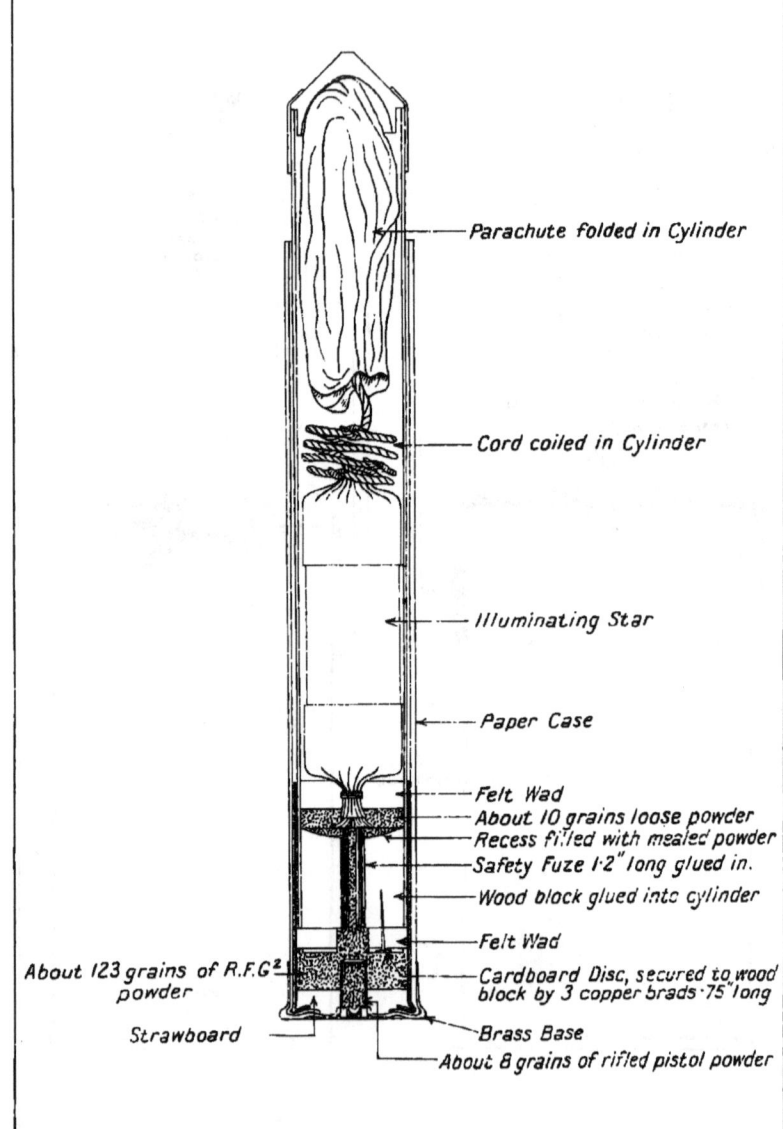

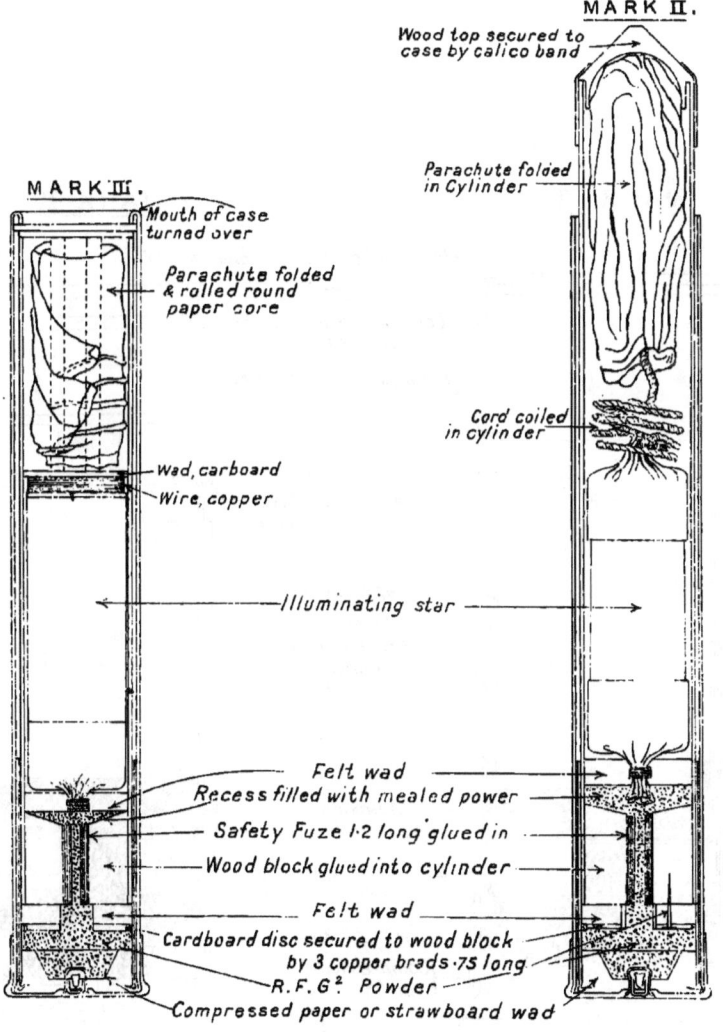

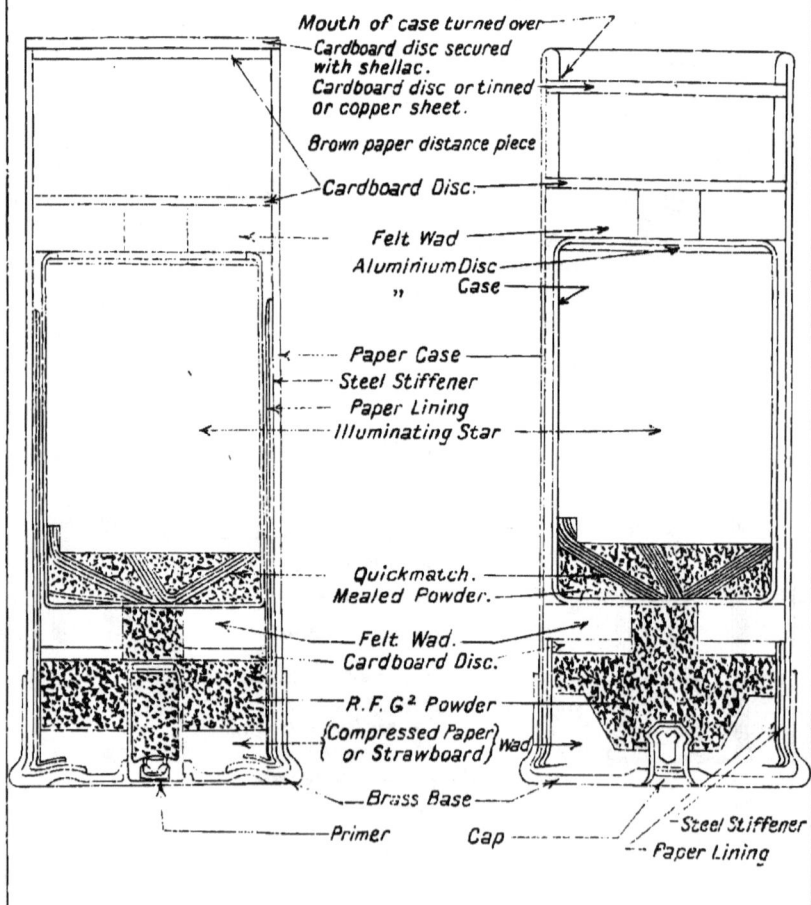

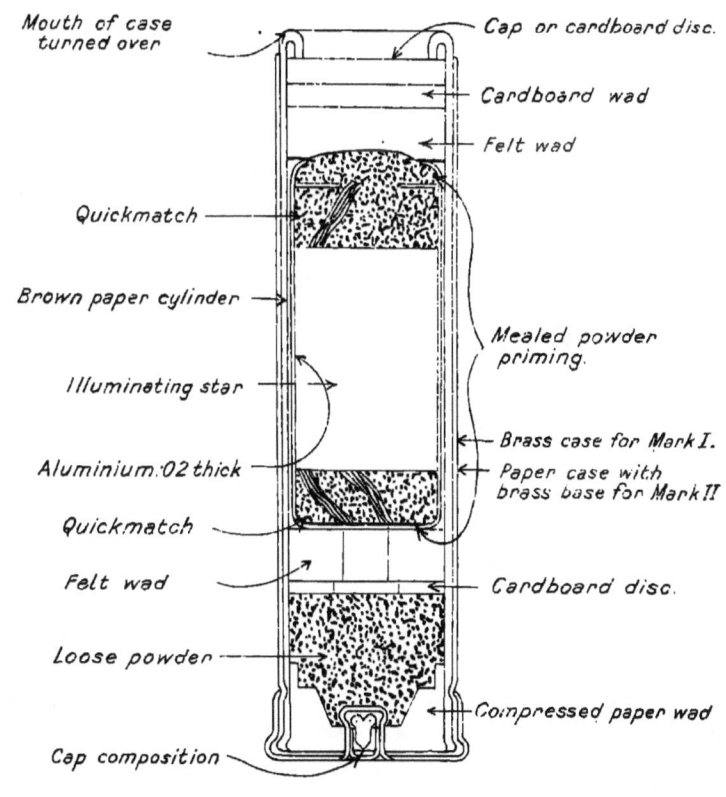

Plate XVIII

CARTRIDGE, SIGNAL, 1½ INCH, WHITE.
SCALE 1/1.

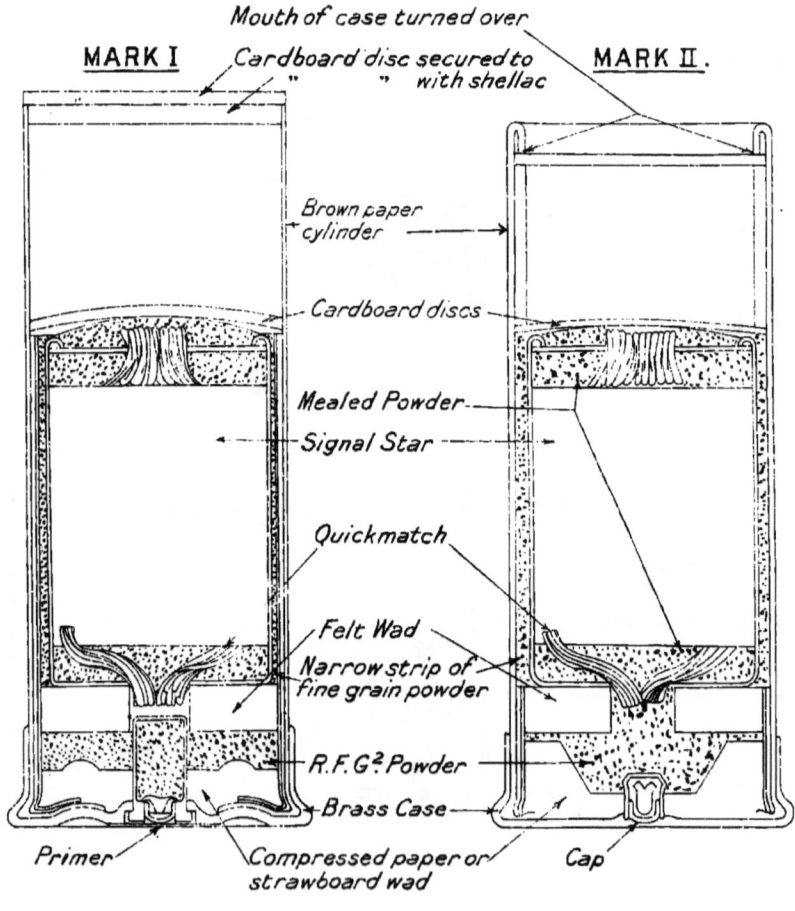

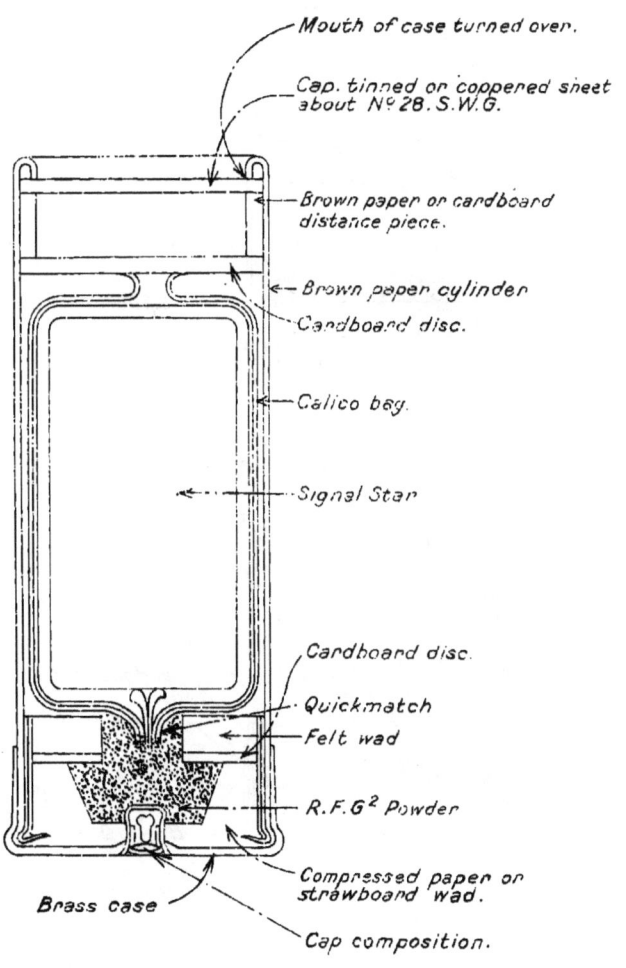

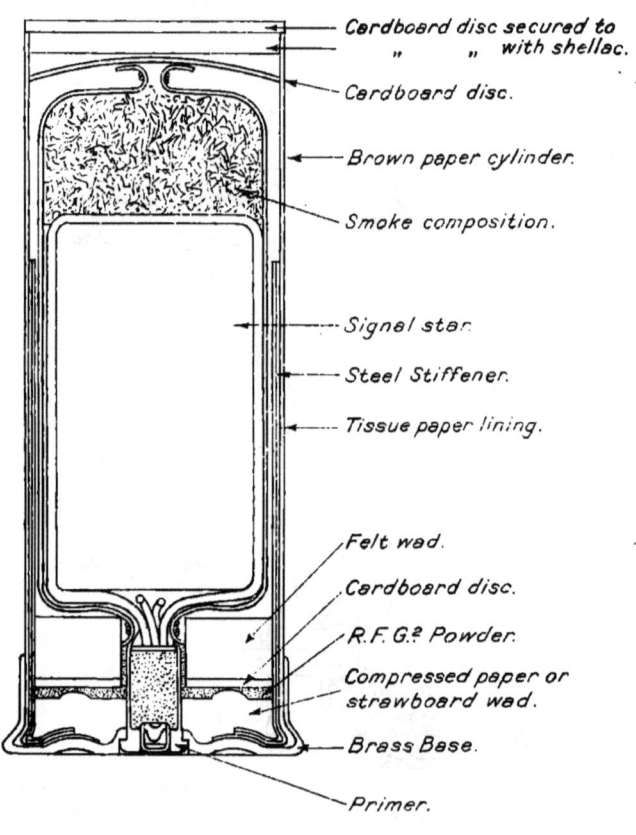

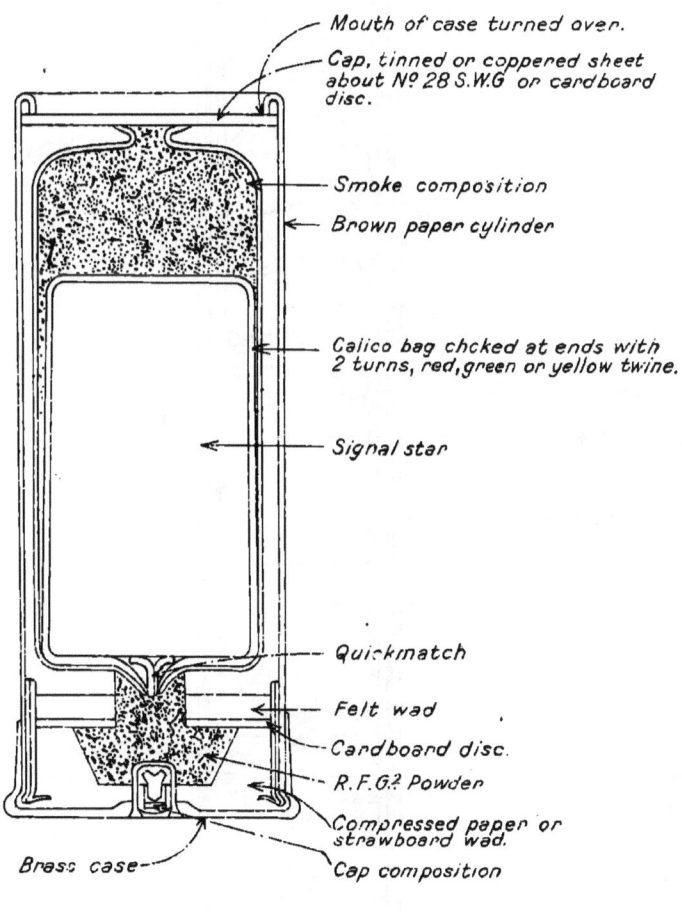

Plate XXII.

CARTRIDGE, SIGNAL 1½ INCH PARACHUTE CHANGING WHITE TO {RED, MARK I. / GREEN, MARK I.

- Mouth of case turned over
- Card wad closing cylinder
- " " " cart^{ge} case
- Cylinder
- Parachute
- Paper tube
- Parachute strings coiled
- Copper wire coiled
- Coloured flare composition
- Flare case
- White flare composition
- Quickmatch
- Opening charge black powder
- Time Fuze
- Propellant
- Card Wad
- Felt Wad
- Card Wad
- Wood Base
- Felt Wad
- Card Wad

Malby & Sons, Lith.

CARTRIDGE, SIGNAL, 1½ INCH, WITH PARACHUTE AND COLOURED SMOKE, MARK I.
FOR USE FROM AIRCRAFT.

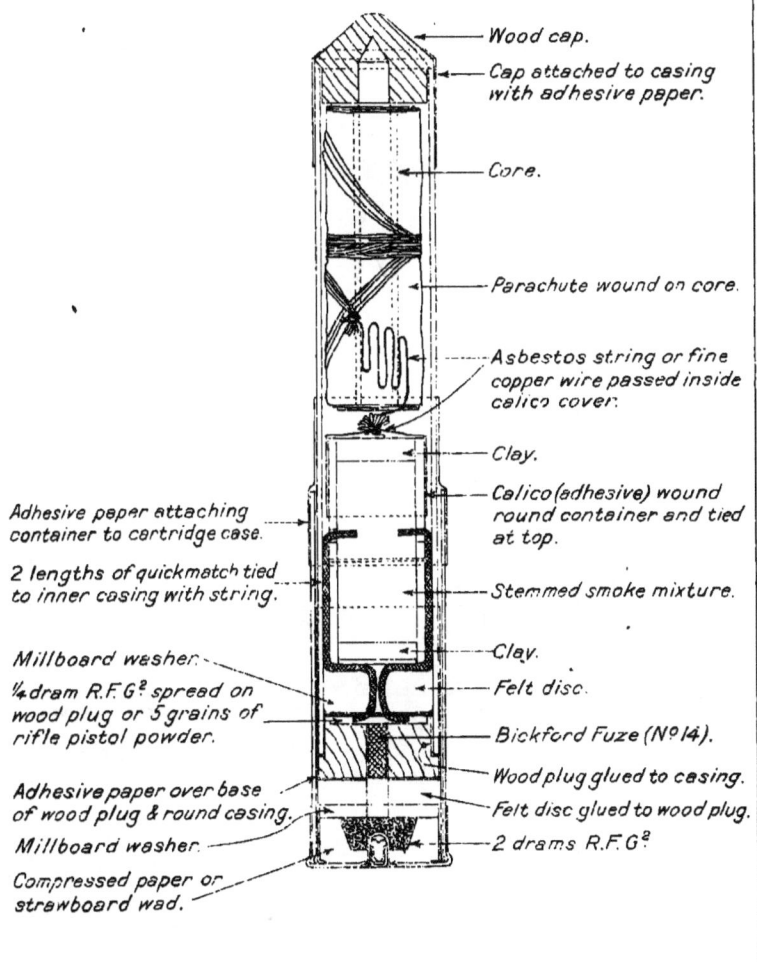

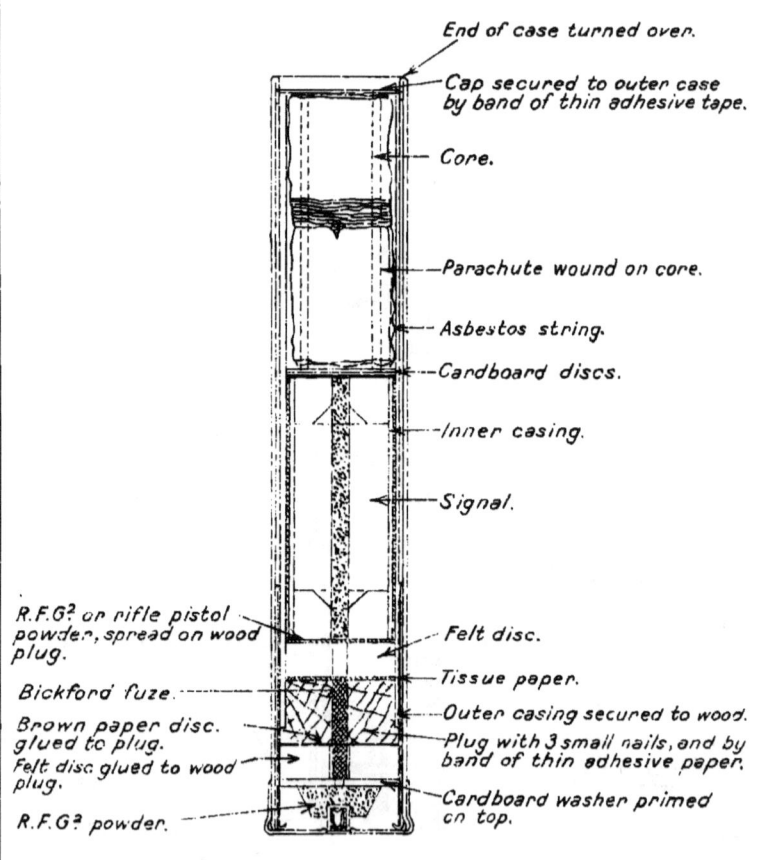

Plate XXV.

CARTRIDGE SIGNAL 1½ INCH, WITH CHANGING COLOUR STAR, MARK I.
SCALE ⅟₁.

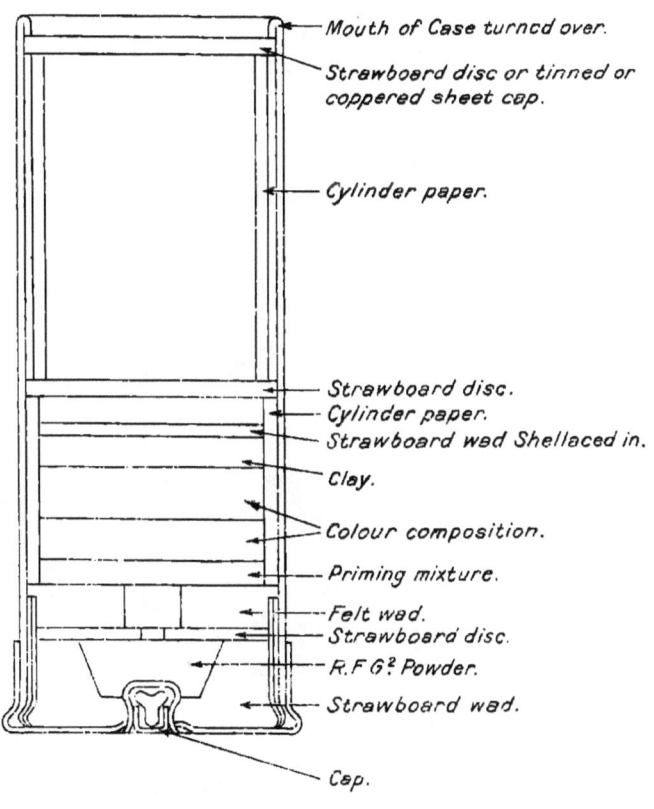

Plate XXVI

CARTRIDGE, SIGNAL, 1½ INCH, THREE STAR, DARK IGNITION, MARKS I AND II.

SCALE 1/1

MARK I.—PAPER CASE WITH BRASS BASE.
MARK II.—SOLID DRAWN BRASS CASE.

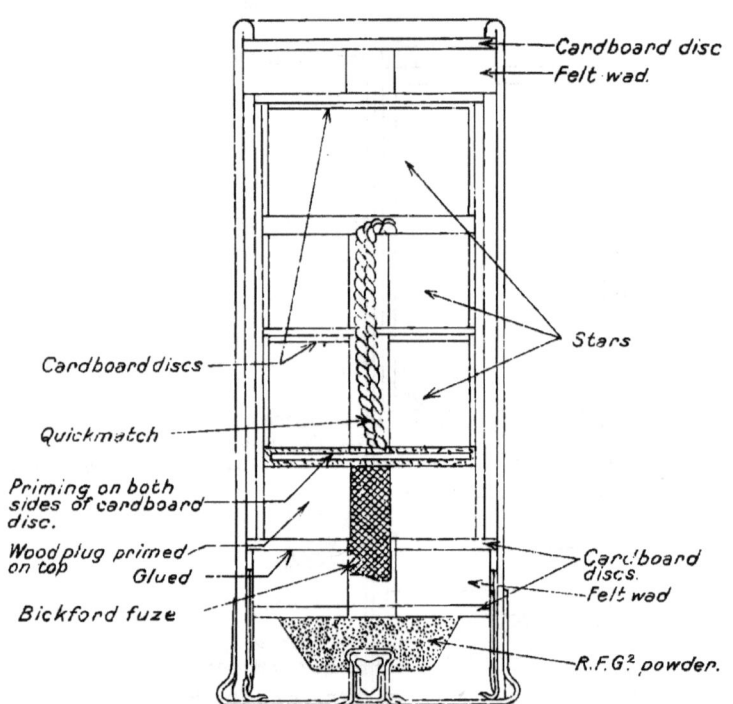

ALTERNATIVE METHOD OF CLOSING.

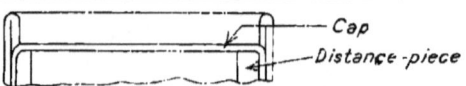

Plate XXVII

CARTRIDGE, SIGNAL, 1½ INCH, WITH SCINTILLATING STAR M^{ks} I & II.

Scale ⅟₁.

Mark I :- Paper case with Brass base.
Mark II :- Solid drawn brass case.

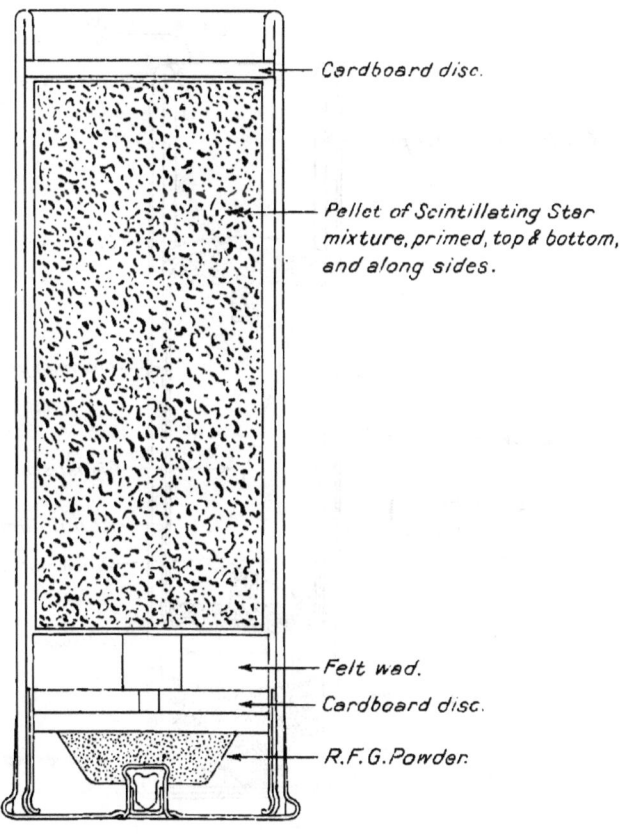

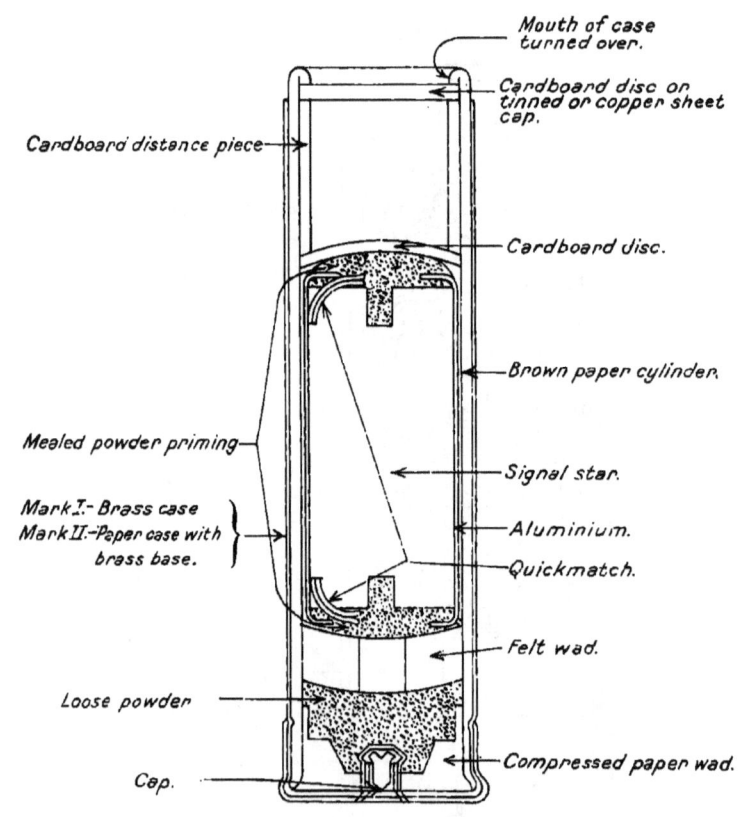

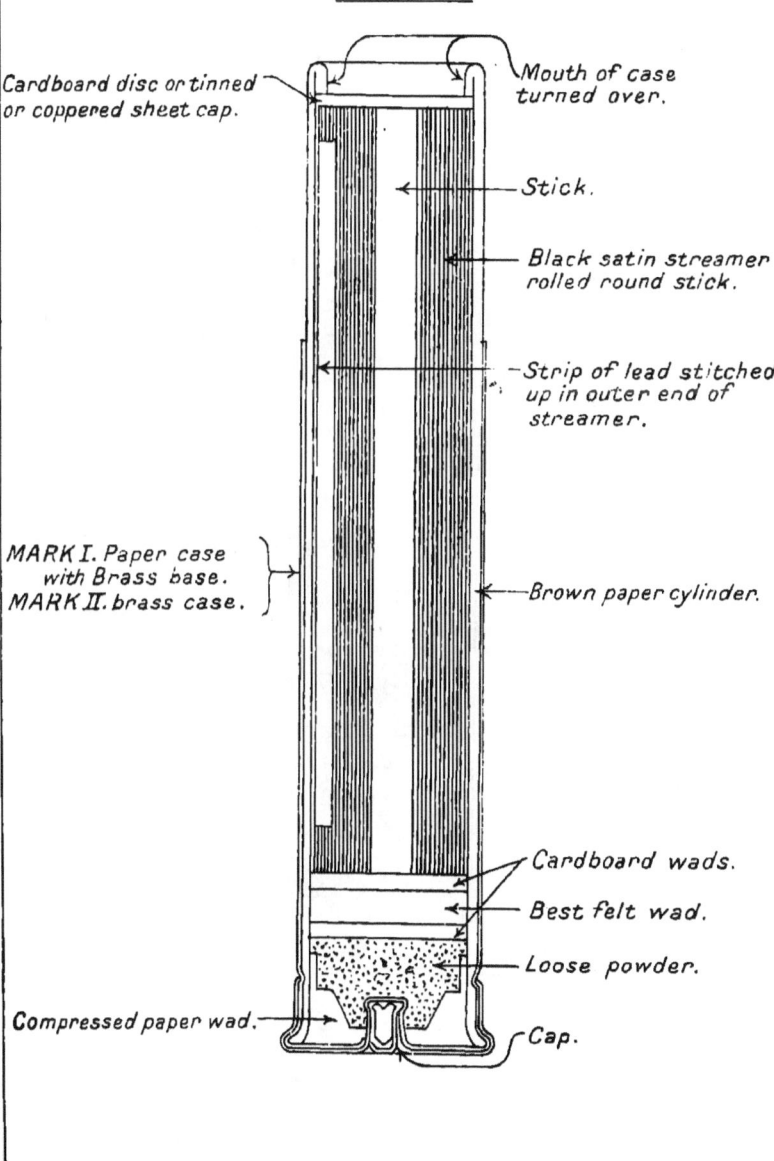

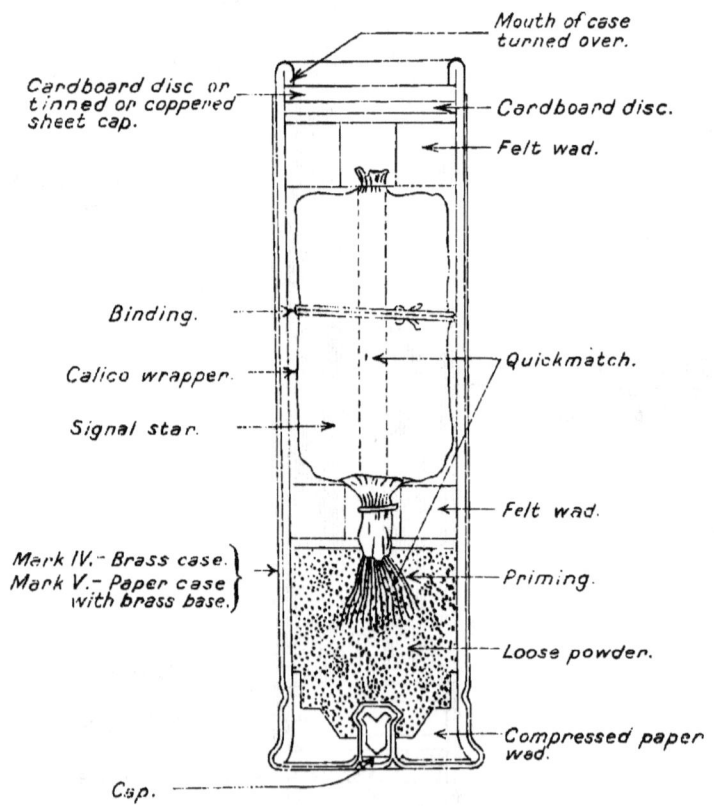

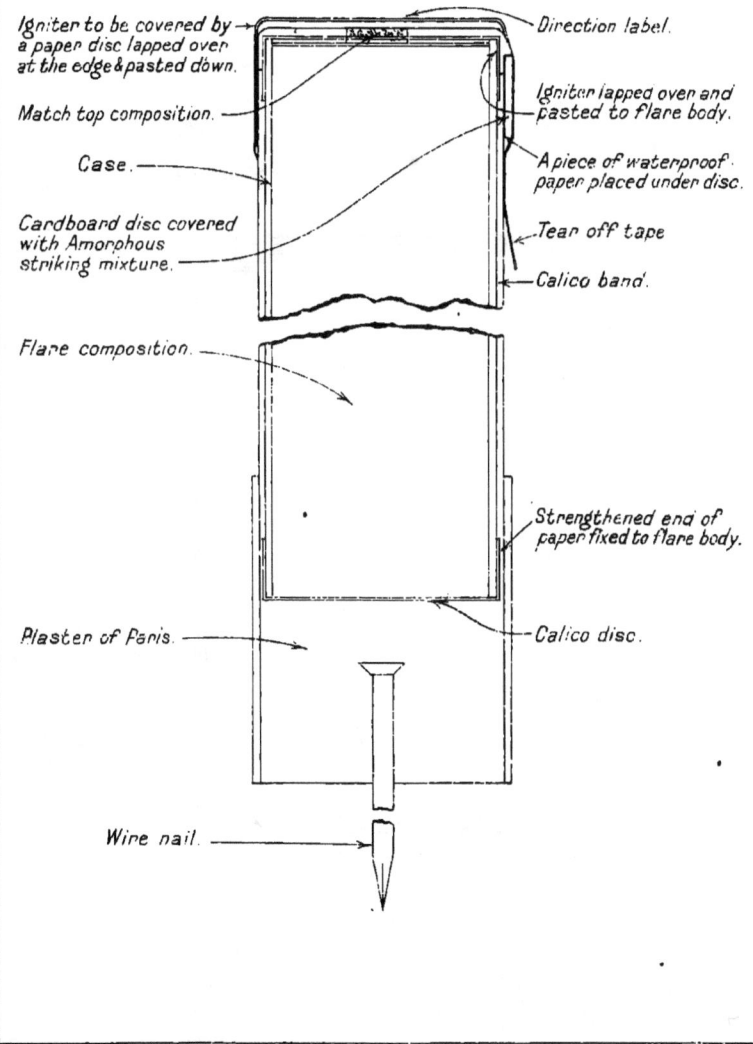

Plate XXXII

FLARES, GROUND, { RED, GREEN, YELLOW, WHITE.

3 INCHES LONG BY 2 INCHES DIAMETER MARK I.
1¾ INCHES LONG BY 2 INCHES DIAMETER MARK I.
1½ INCHES LONG BY 1½ INCHES DIAMETER MARK I.

TYPICAL

Igniter to be covered by a paper disc lapped over at the edge, and pasted to case.

Igniter lapped over.

Direction label.

Striking disc.

Calico band.

A piece of waterproof paper placed under disc.

Case.

Tear off band.

Calico band lapped over and pasted.

Flare composition.

Malby & Sons. Lith.

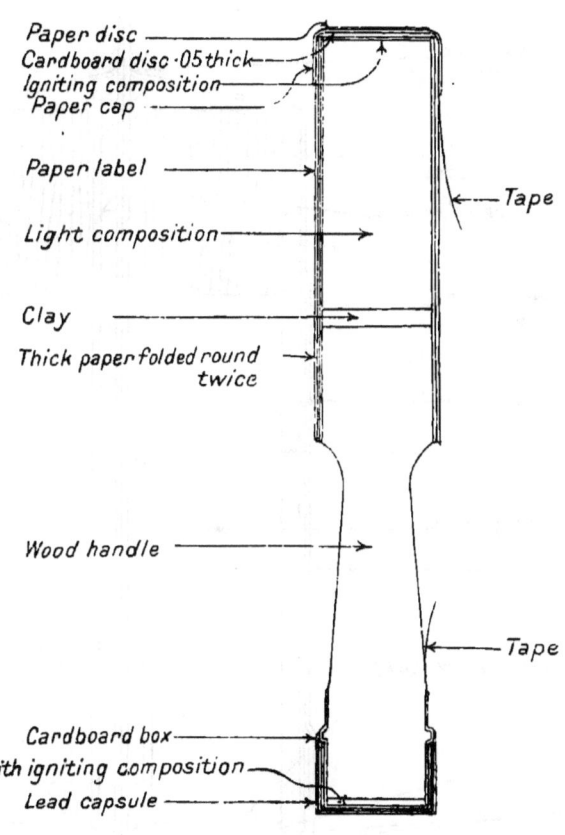

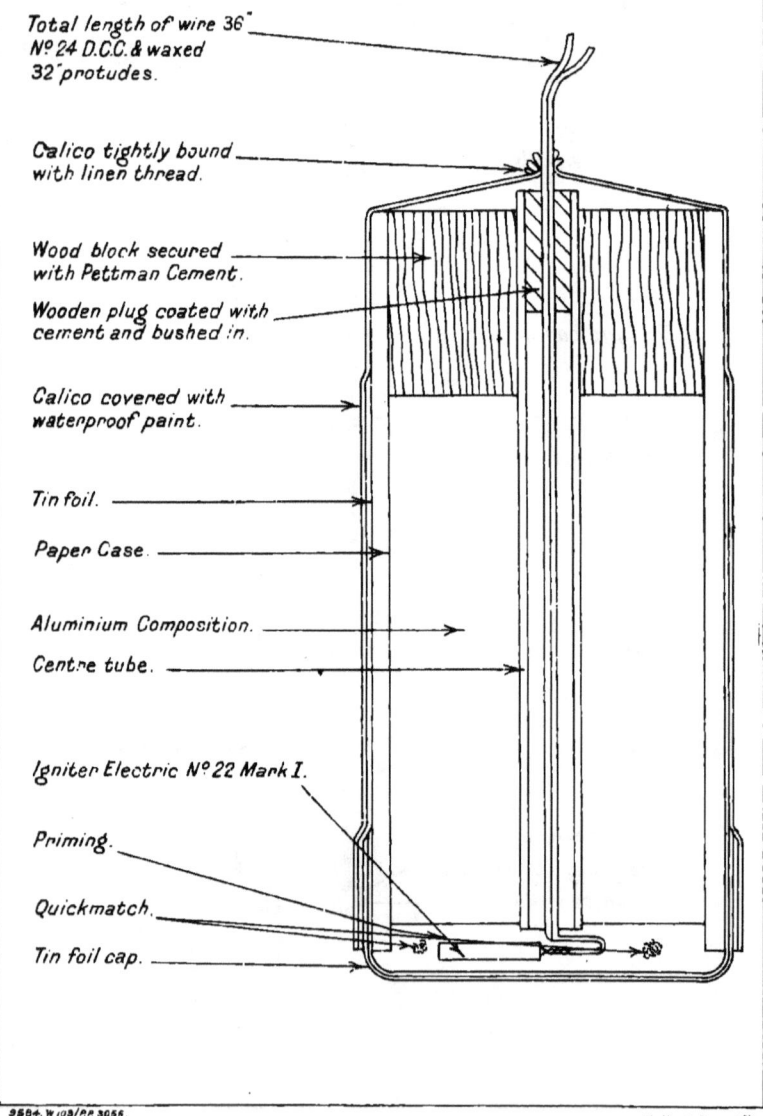

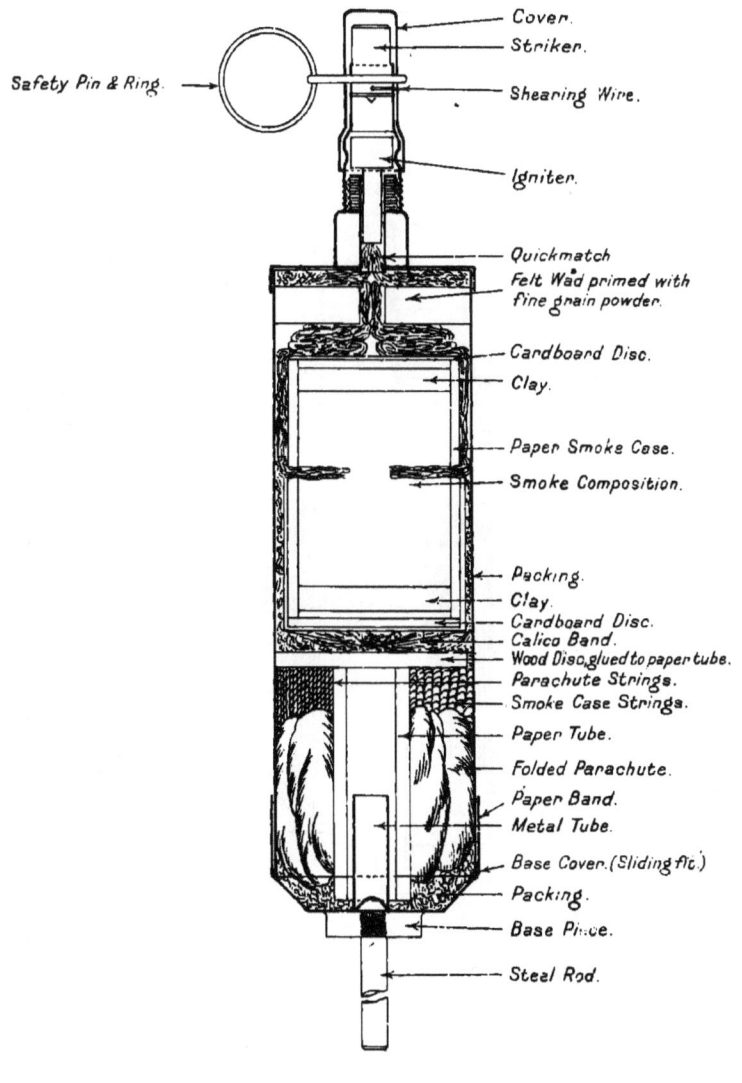

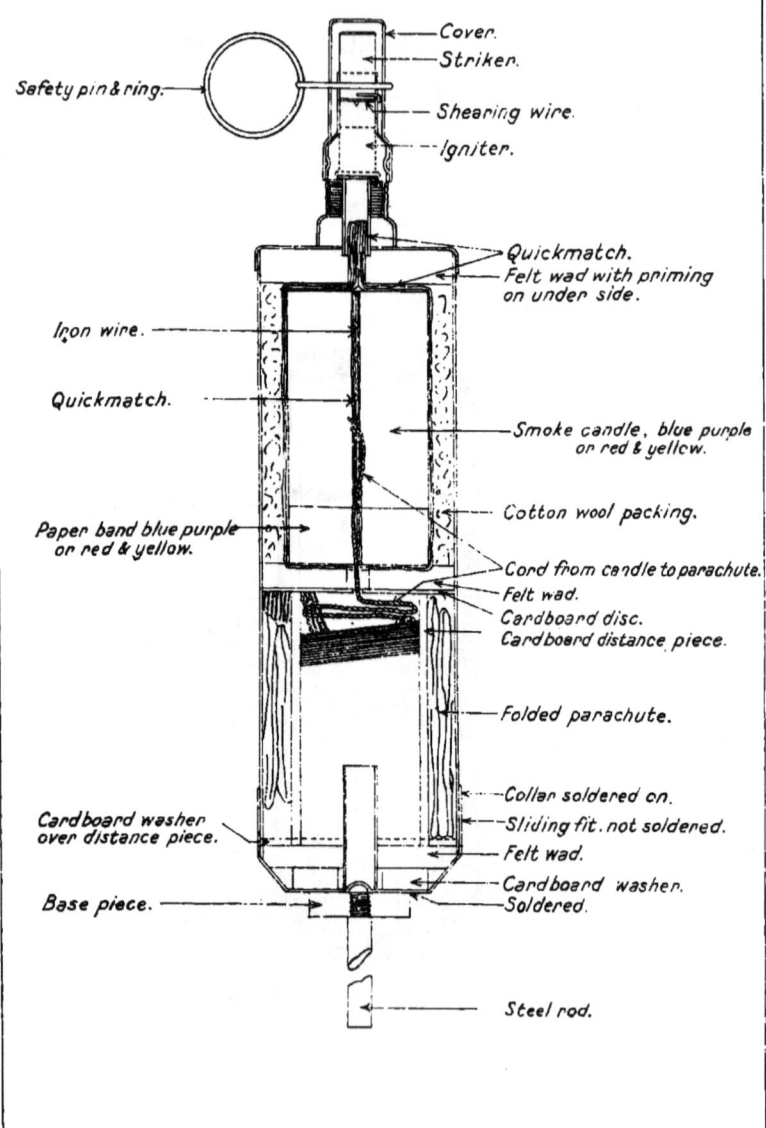

Plate XXXVII.

GRENADE, ·303 RIFLE No. 32 NIGHT SIGNAL MK. II.

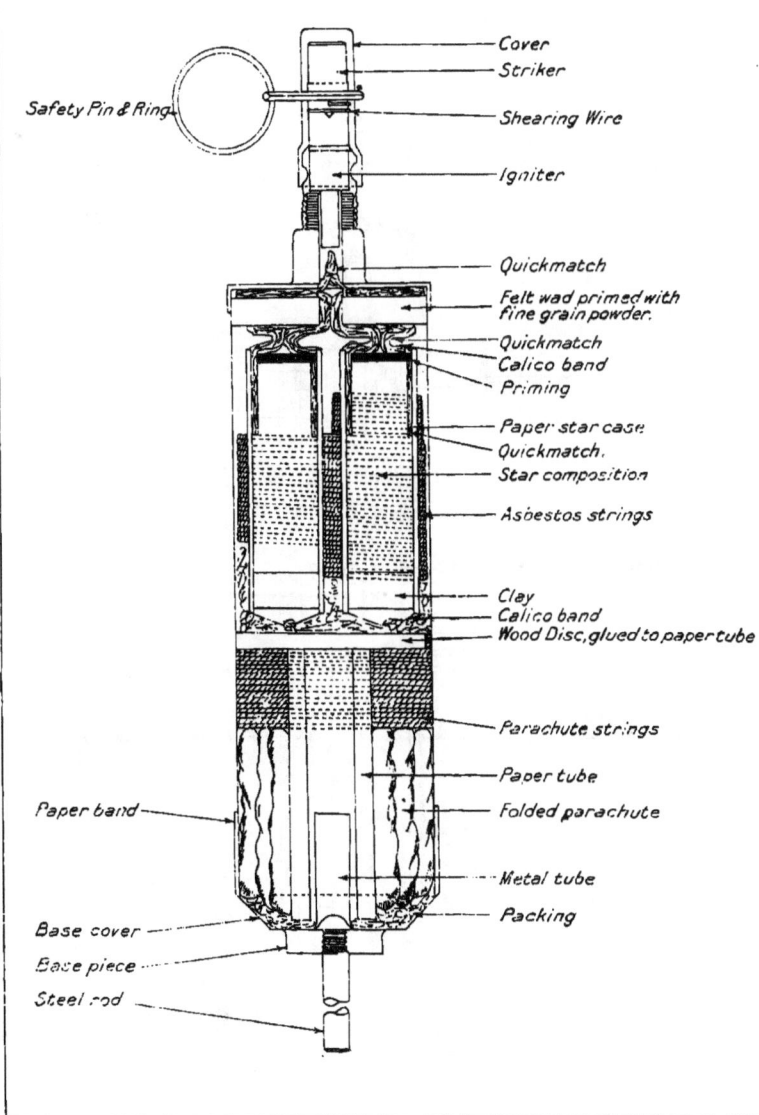

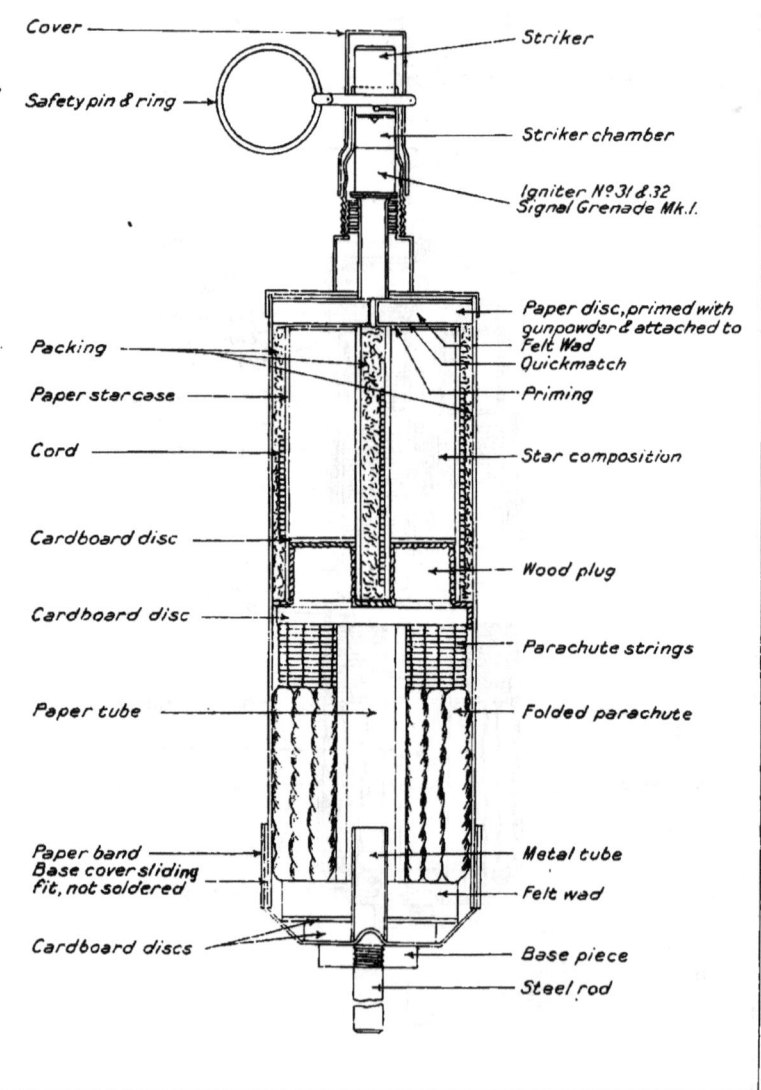

Plate XXXIX.

GRENADE, ·303 INCH RIFLE, N° 38 NIGHT SIGNAL MARK II.
Scale ½.

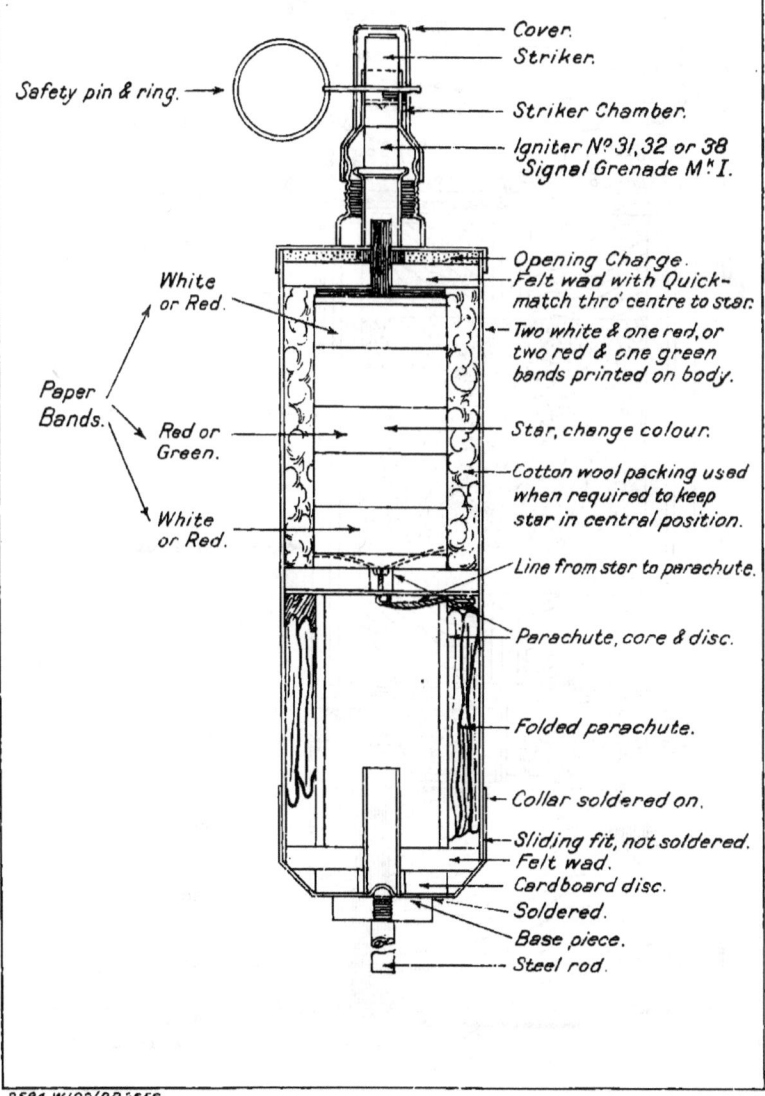

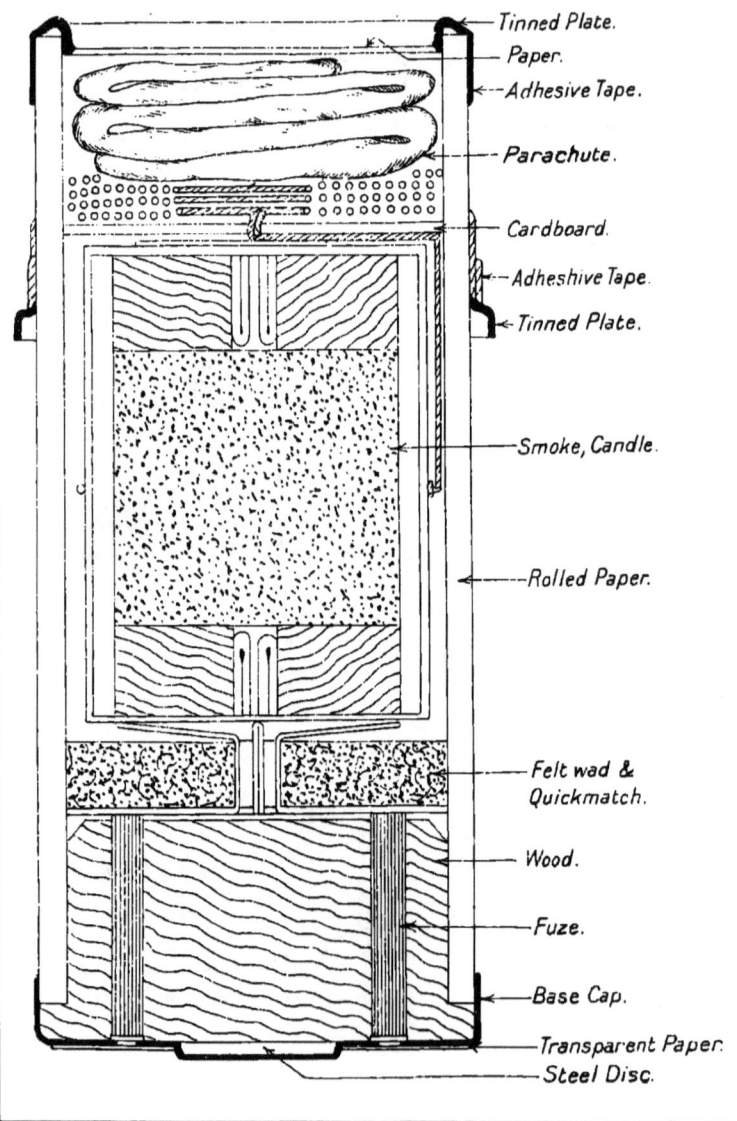

Plate XLI.

GRENADE, 303 INCH RIFLE N.º 45.
NIGHT SIGNAL MARK I.
SCALE ½.

- Label
- Tinned Plate
- Adhesive Tape
- Black or Tinned Plate
- Cardboard Disc
- Star Composition
- Rolled Paper
- Quickmatch
- Felt Wad
- Paper Disc primed with Gunpowder
- Wood Block
- Brass Cap
- Transparent Paper
- Steel Disc
- Parachute
- Fuze

Malby & Sons. Lith.

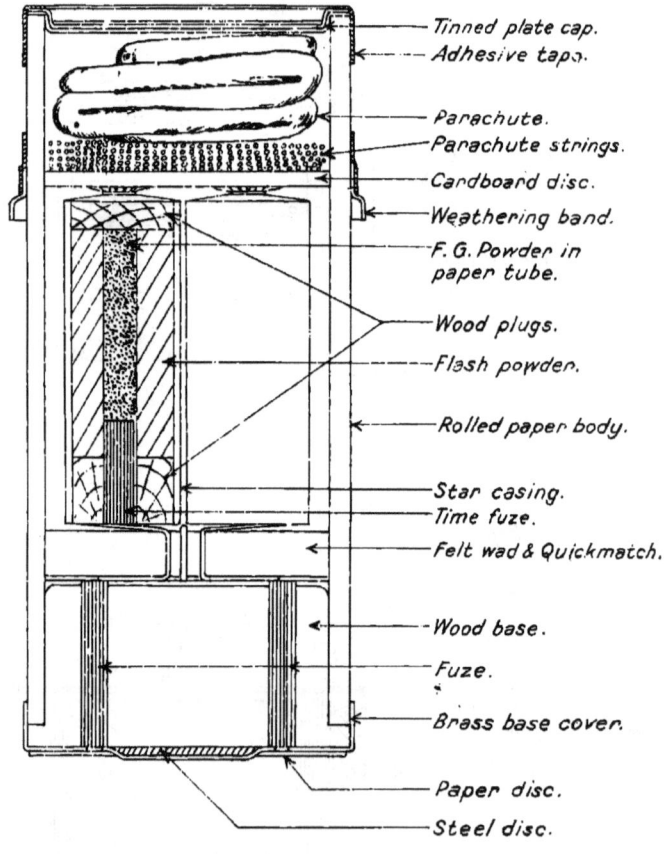

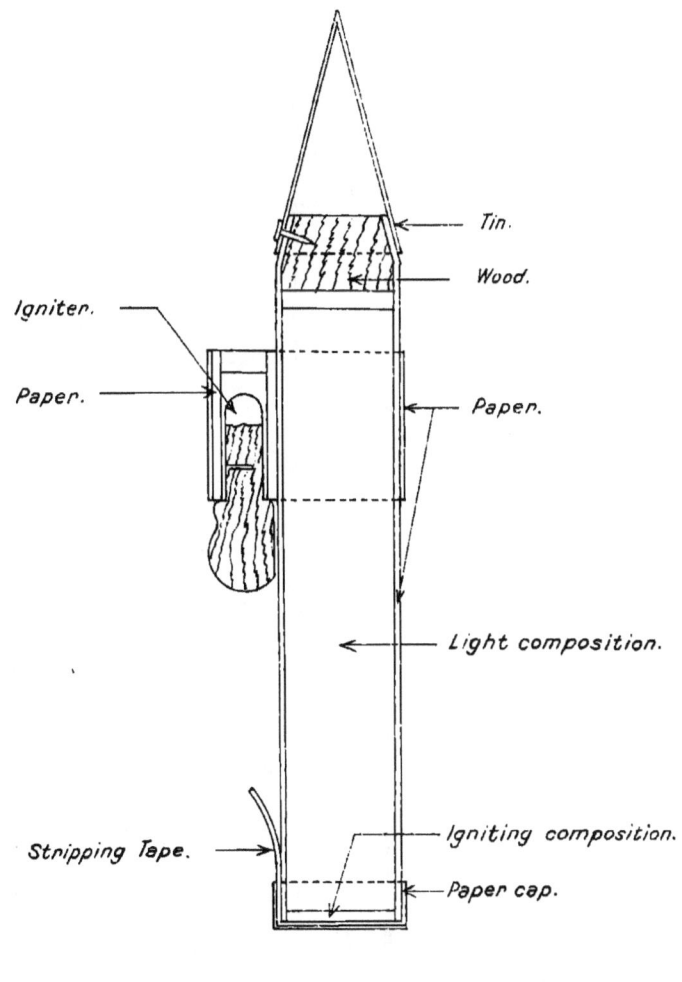

Plate XLIV.

LIGHT ILLUMINATING WRECKS Mark IV.

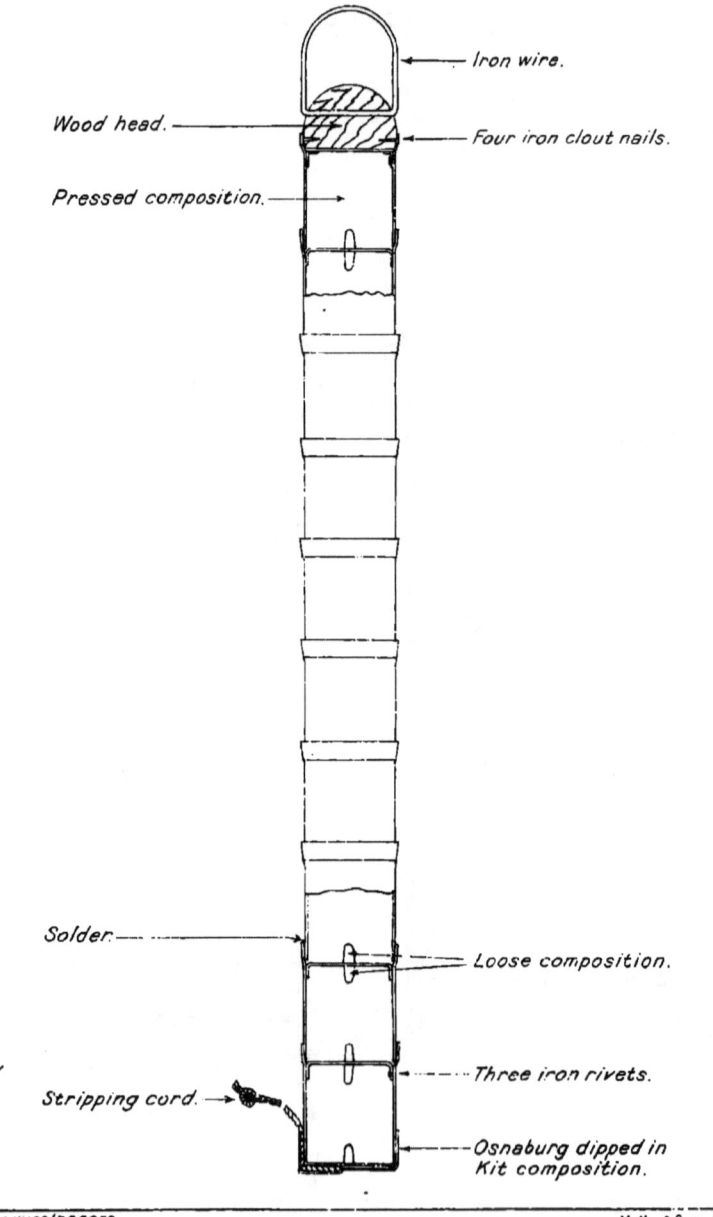

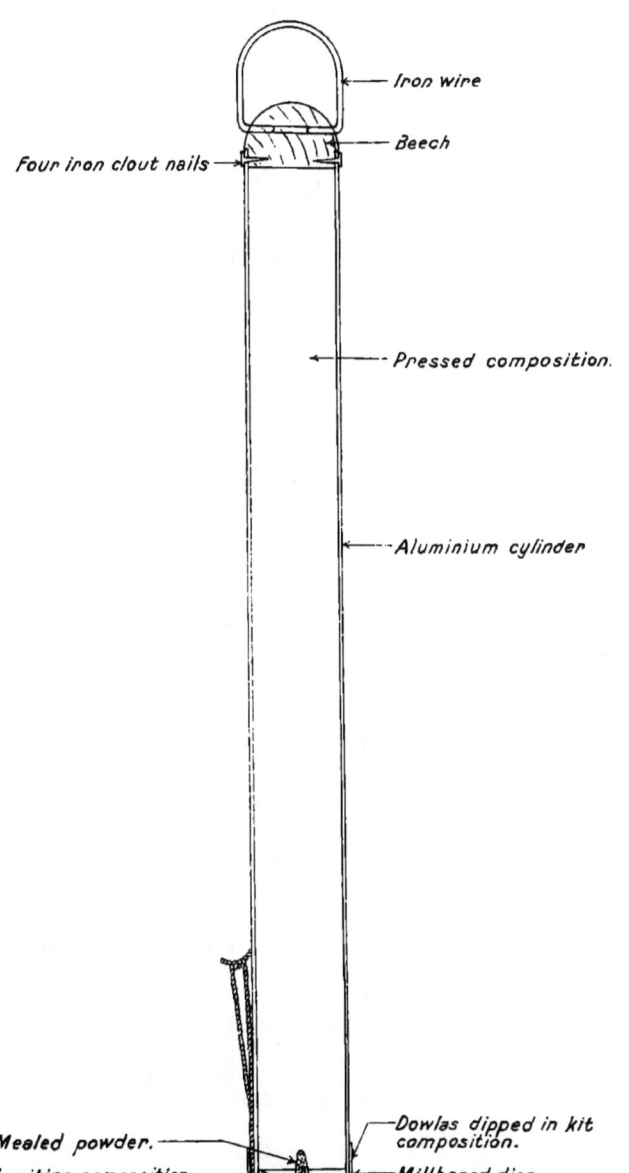

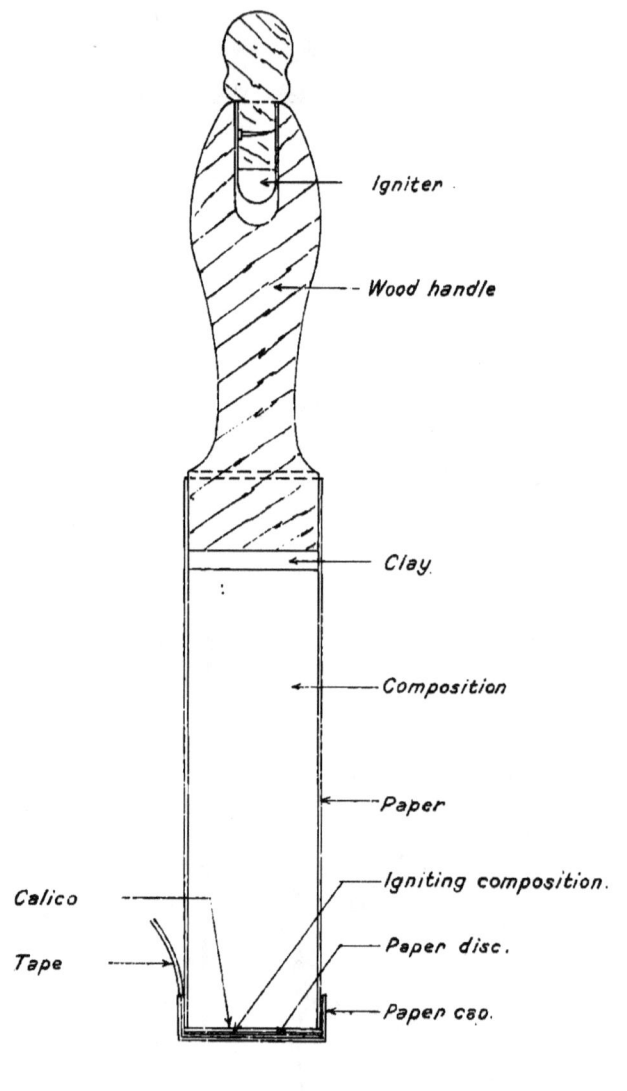

Plate XLVII.

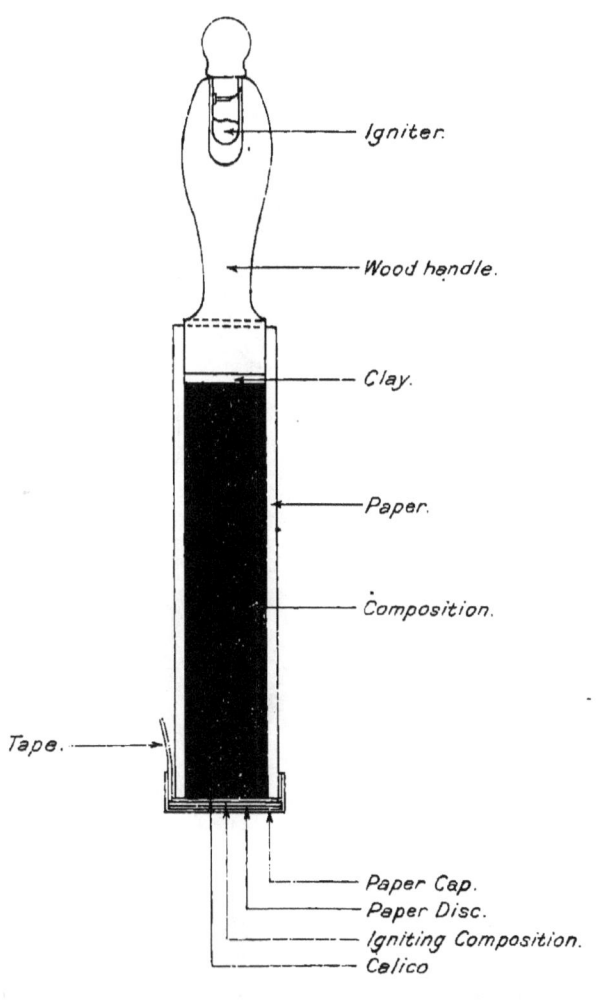

Plate XLVIII.

LIGHT, SHORT, G.S. MARK II.

SCALE ½

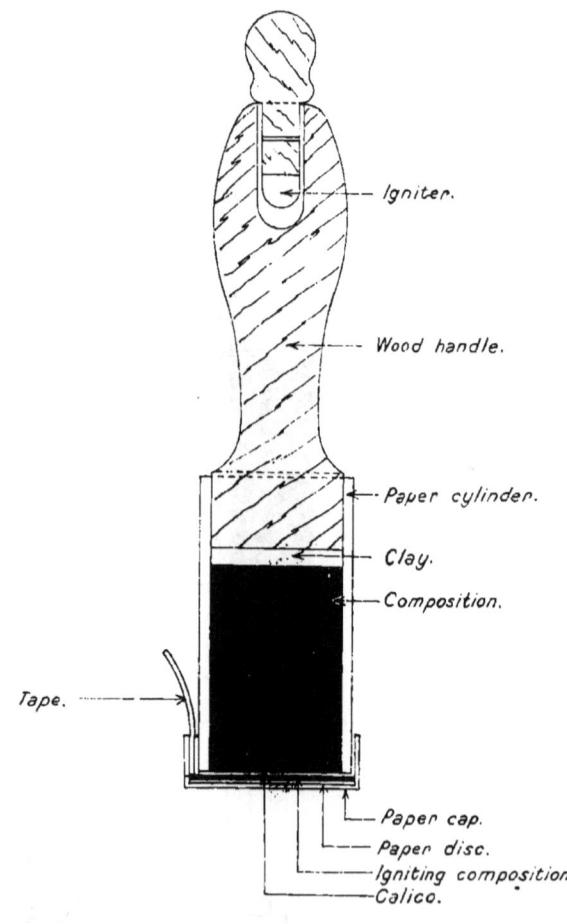

Plate XLIX.

LIGHTS, V.B.S. Mark I.

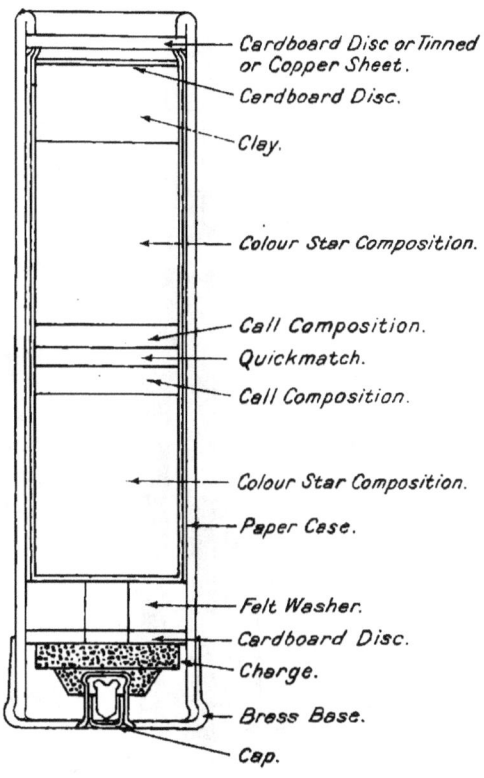

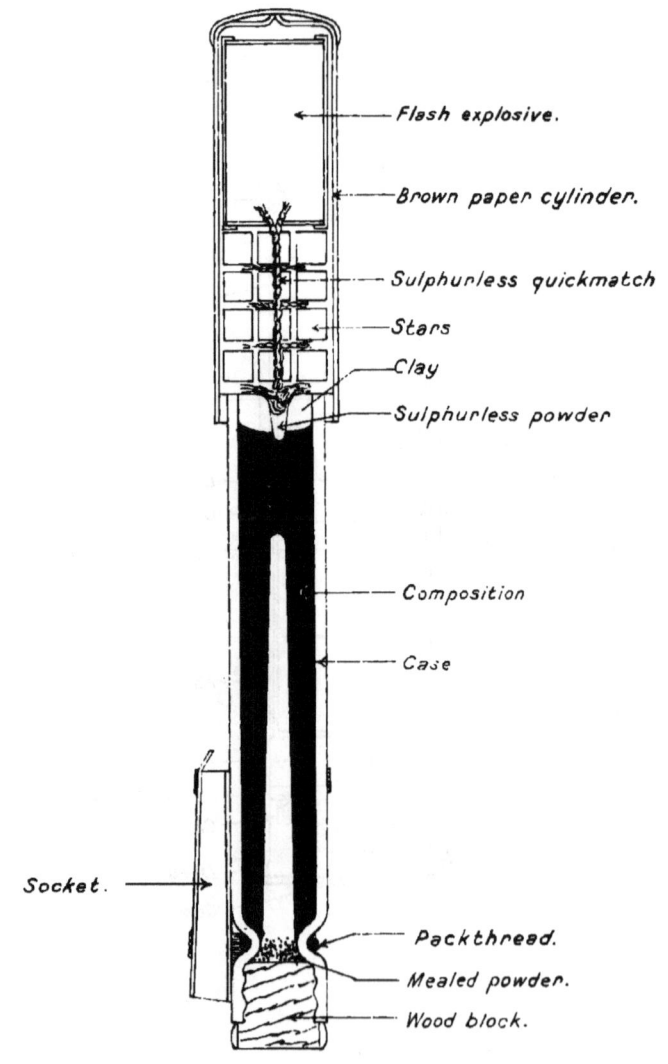

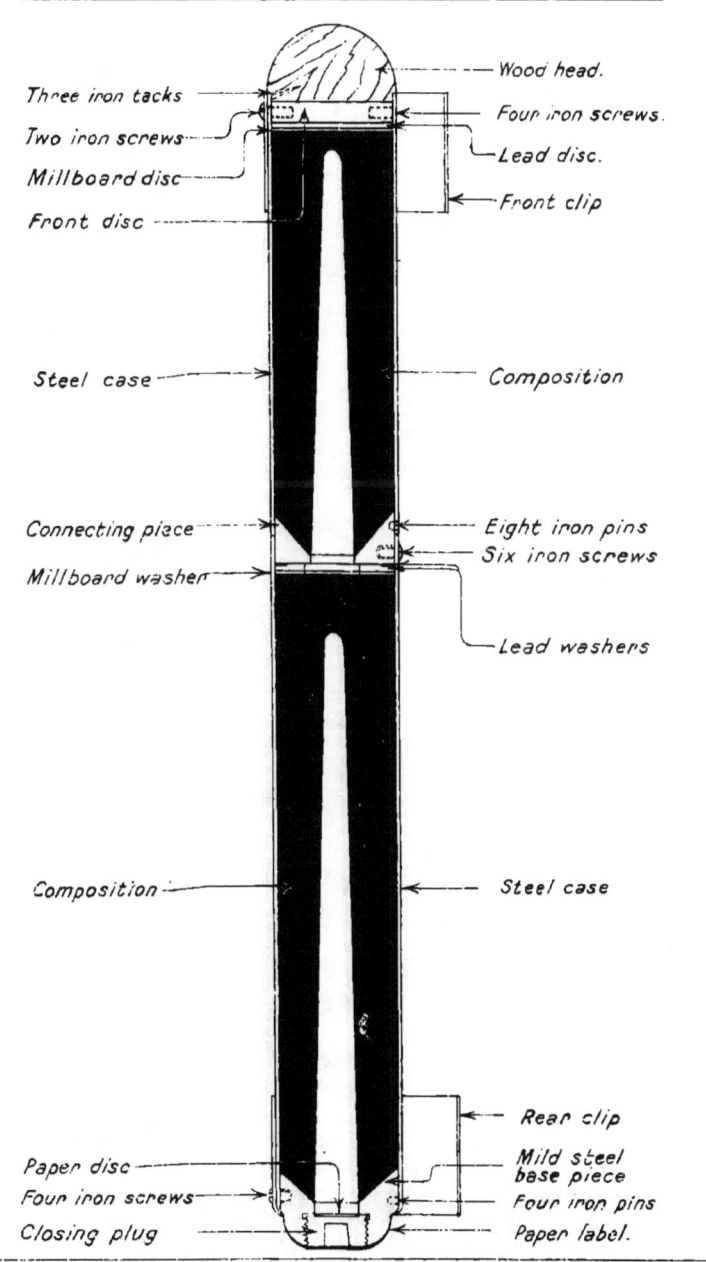

Plate LI.

ROCKET, LIFE SAVING, BOXER, MARK VI.

Plate LII.

ROCKET, LIFE SAVING, BOXER, MARK VI.*

- Three Iron Tacks.
- Two Screws.
- Mild Steel Disc.
- Millboard Disc.
- Wood Block.
- Four Screws.
- Lead Disc.
- Front Clip.
- Composition.
- Millboard Washer.
- Six Screws.
- Lead Washer.
- Lead Washer.
- Composition.
- Case.
- Rear Clip.
- Paper Disc.
- Four Screws.
- Metal Closing Plug.

Malby & Sons. Lith.

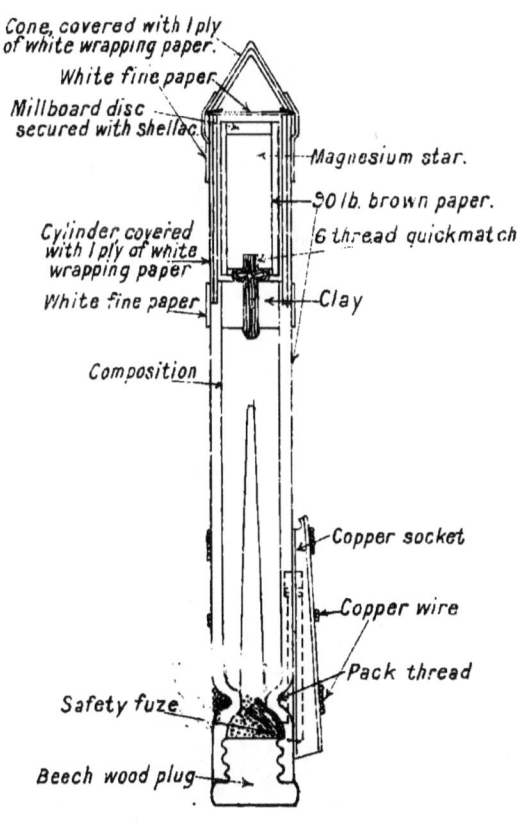

Plate LIV.

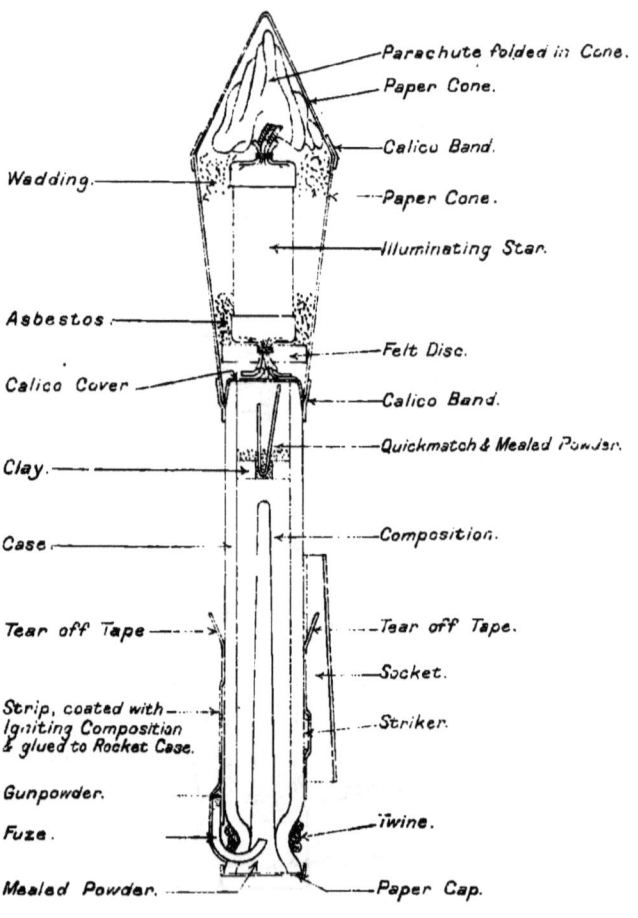

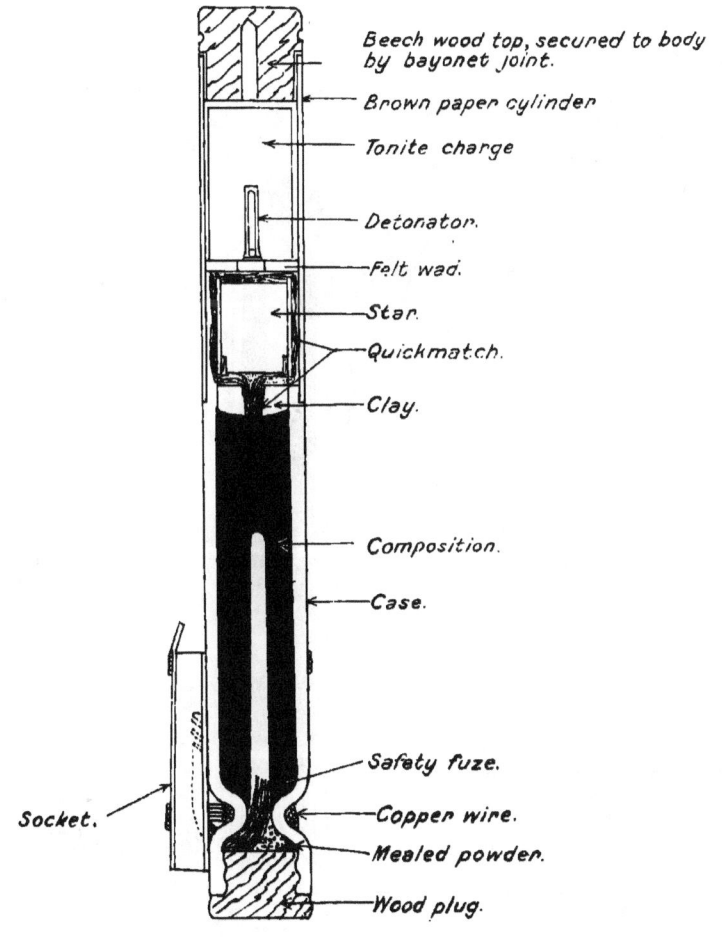

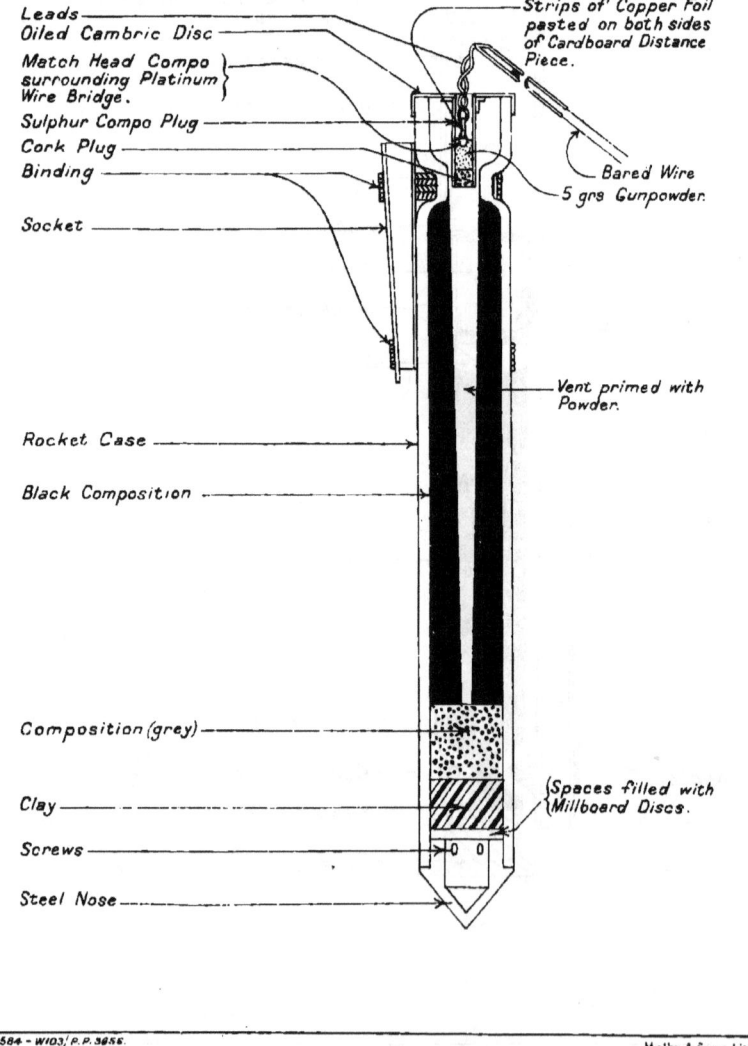

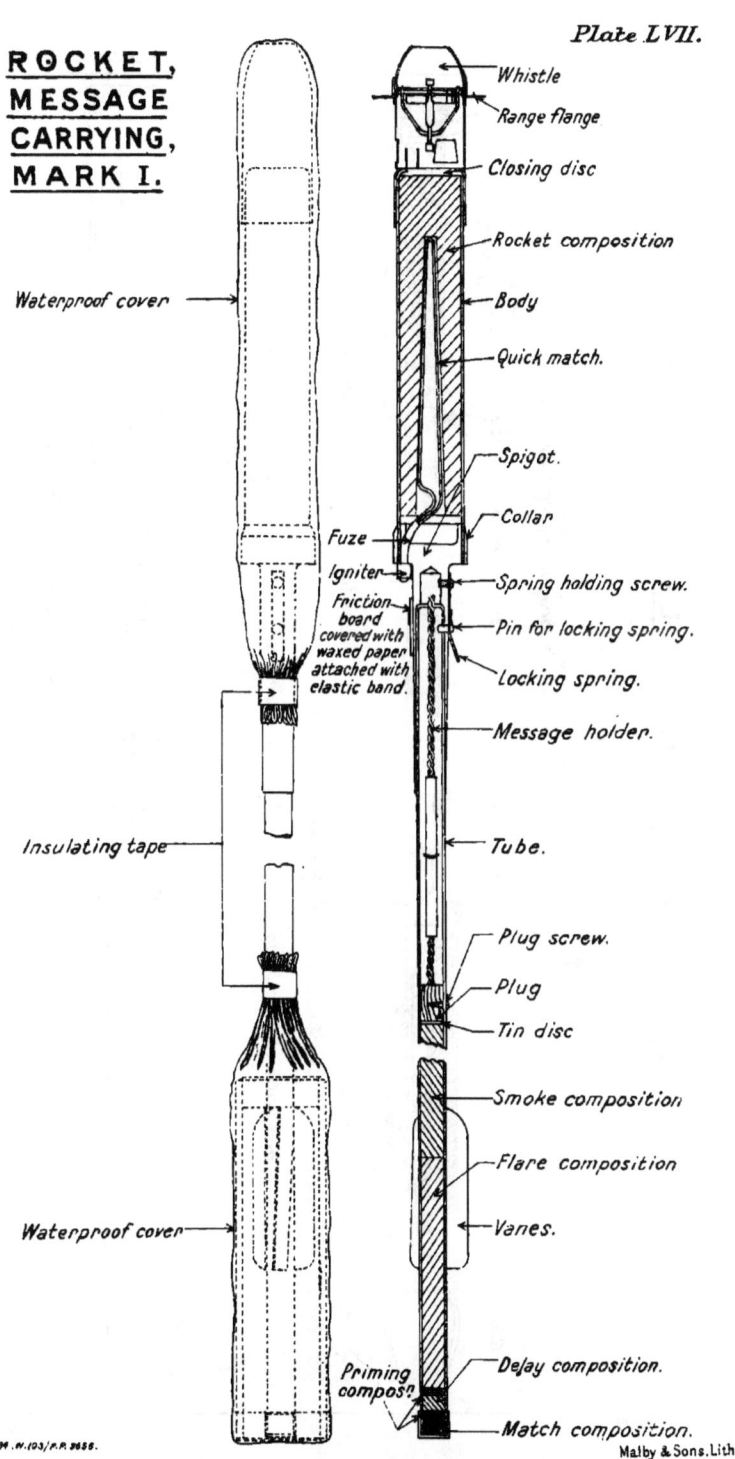

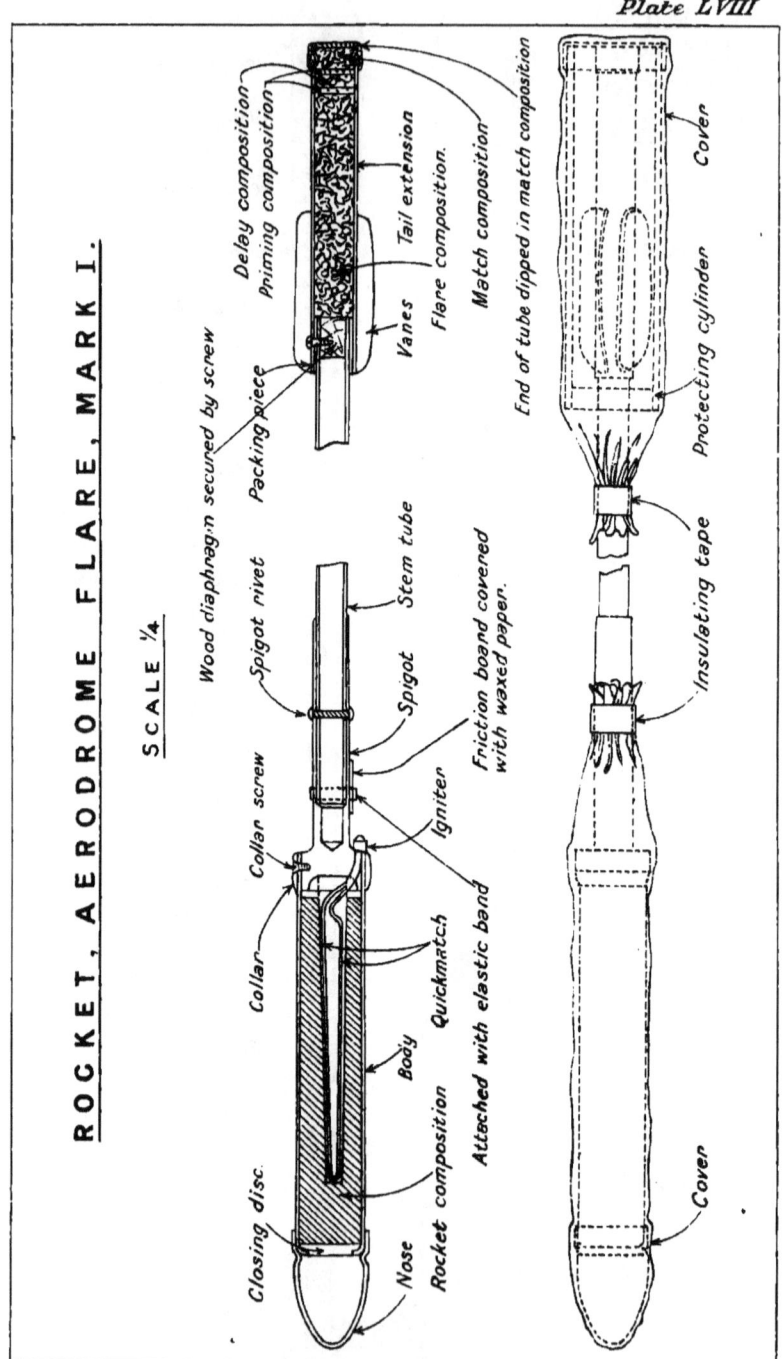

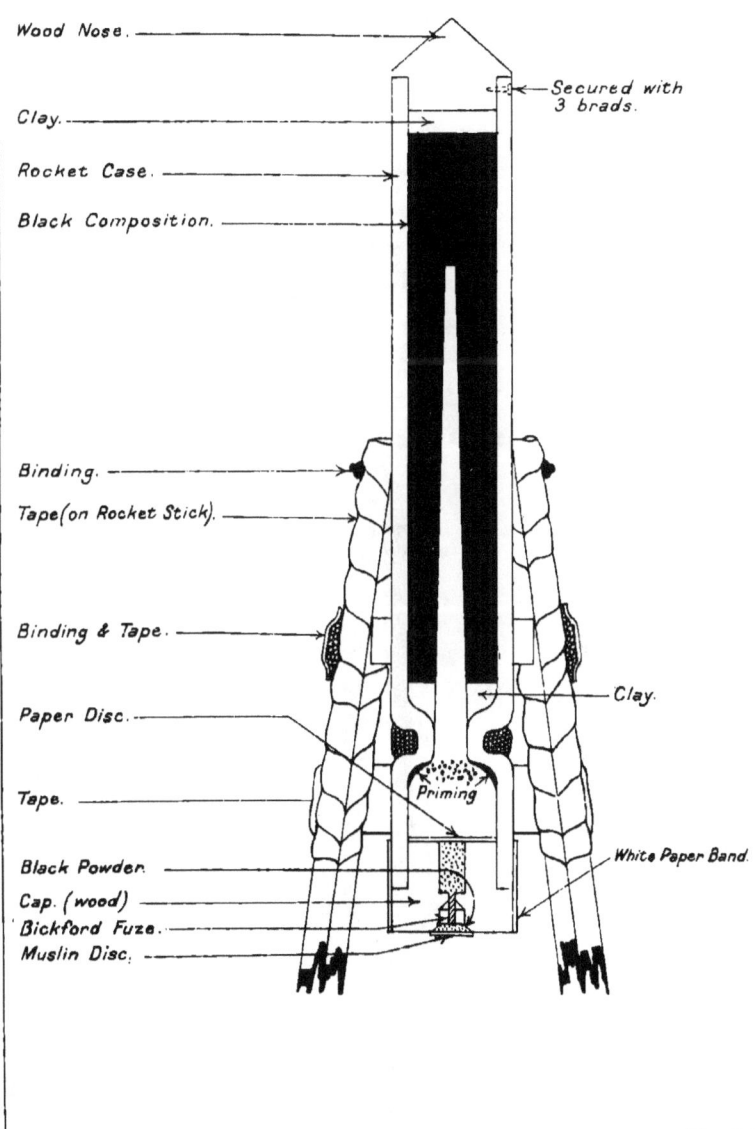

ROCKET SIGNAL 1LB. SERVICE MARK III.
WITHOUT STICK.
SCALE - 1/3

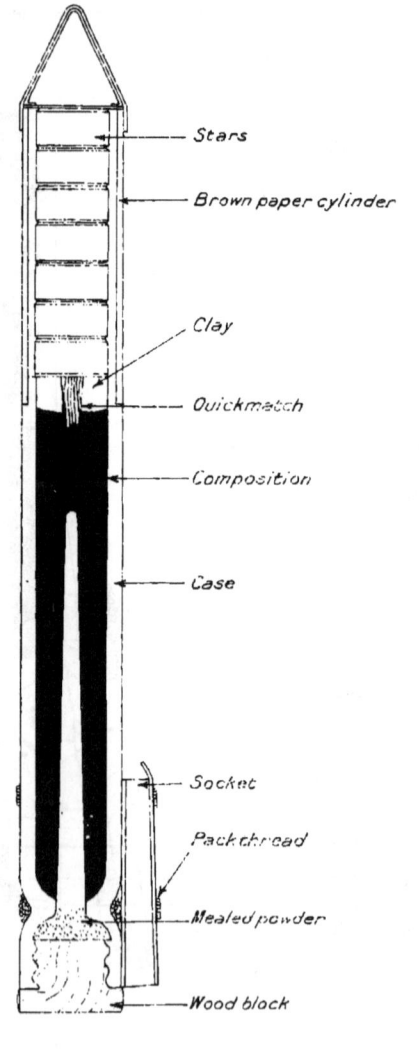

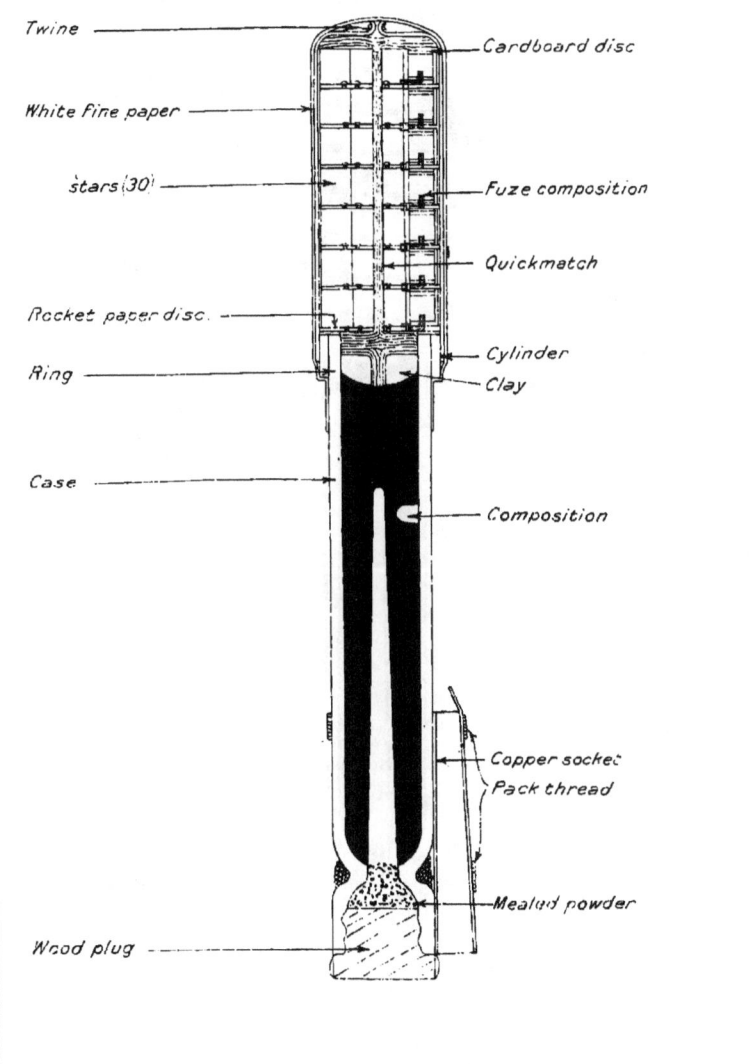

Plate LXI.

Plate LXII.

ROCKET, SIGNAL 1 LB. RED & WHITE MARK II.

SCALE ⅓

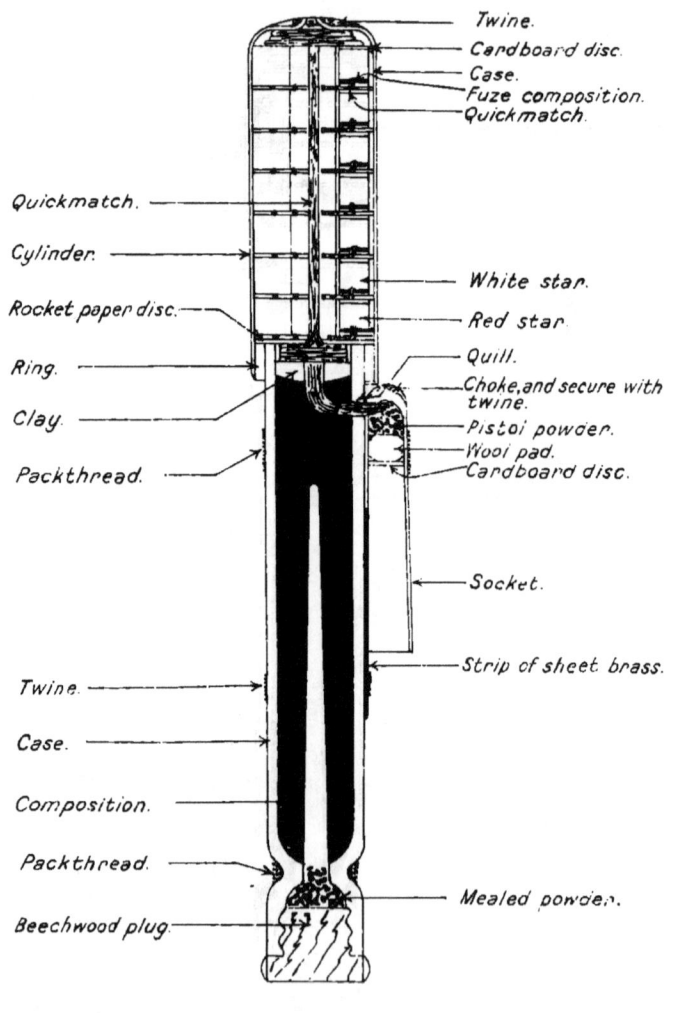

ROCKET, SIGNAL, 1LB., MAGNESIUM "METEOR" {RED/WHITE} MARK I.

ALTERNATIVE HEAD

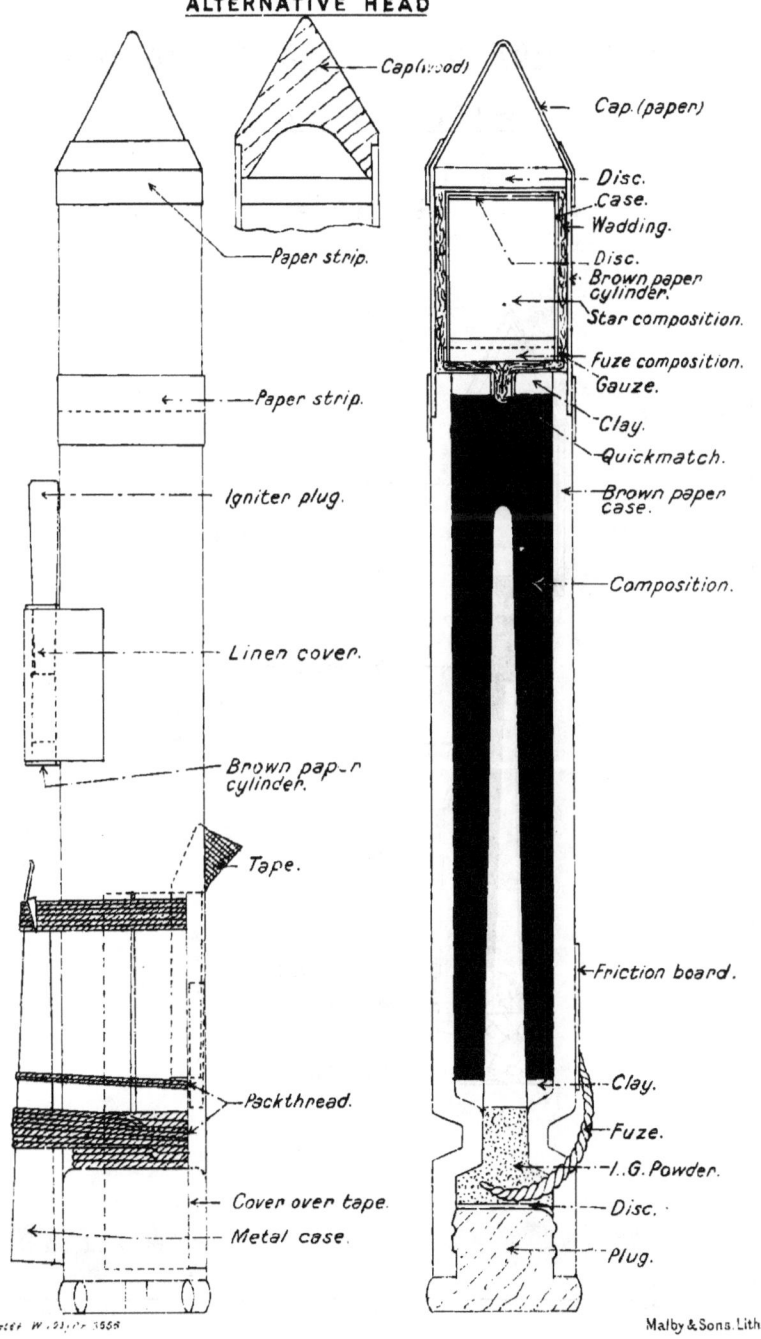

Plate LXIV.

ROCKET, SIGNAL, ½ LB., SERVICE, MARK III.
WITHOUT STICK.

SCALE ⅓

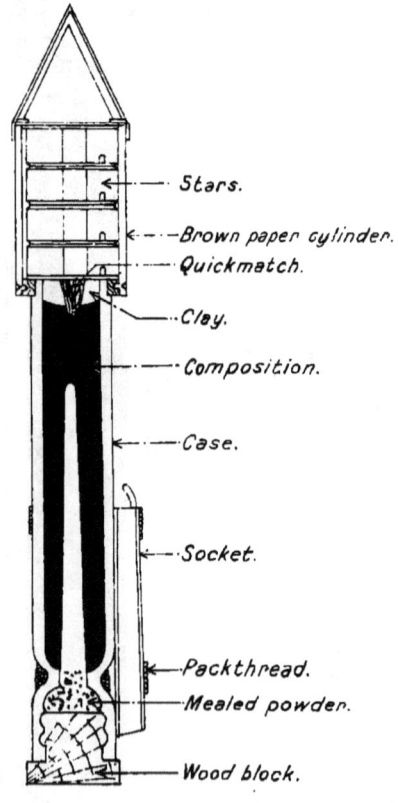

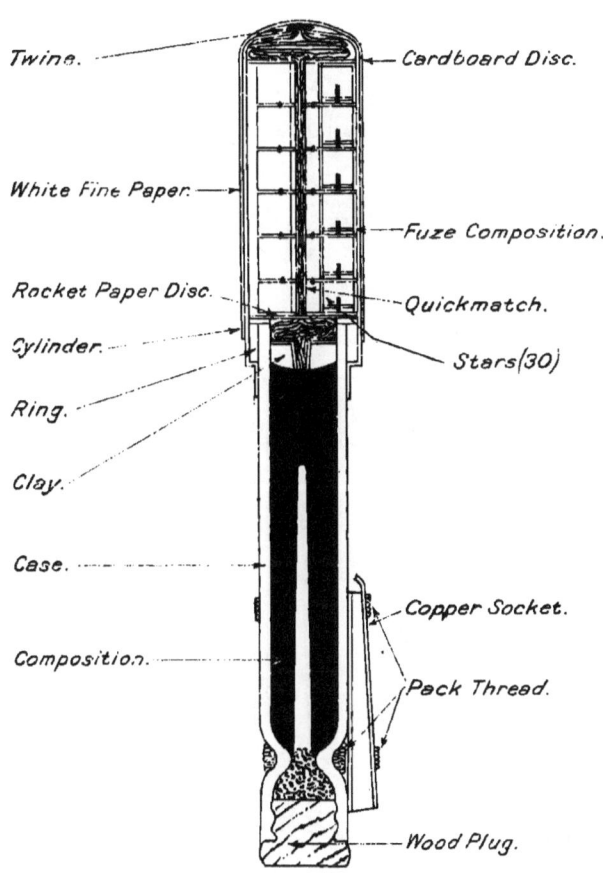

Plate LXVI.

ROCKET, SOUND, ½ LB MARK II.

SCALE ⅓.

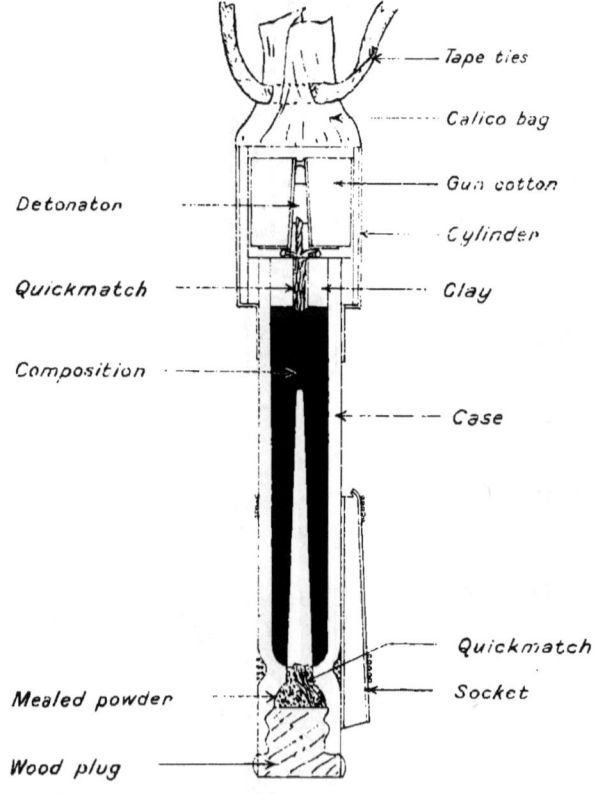

Plate LXVII.

ROCKET SOUND ½ lb. MARK III.
Scale - ⅓.

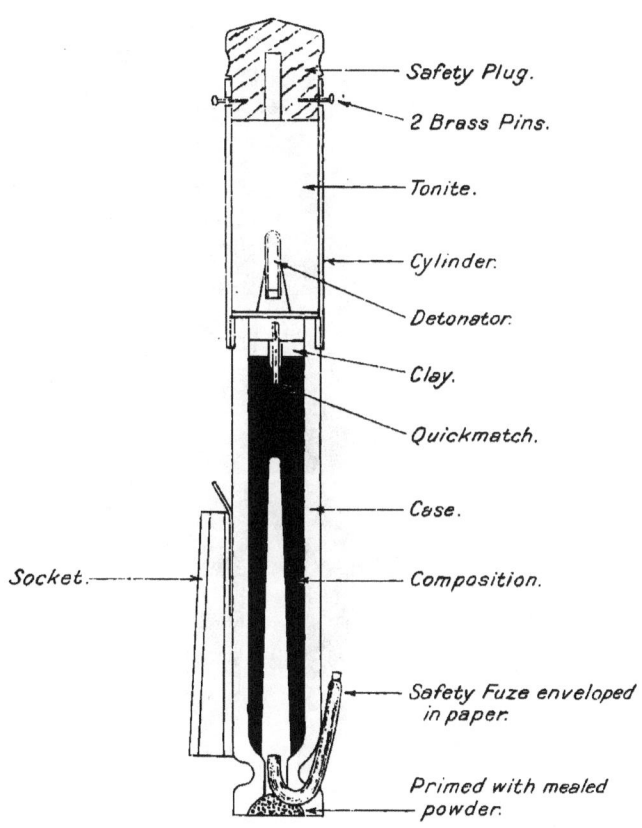

ROCKET, WAR, 24 PR., MARK VII.

SCALE ¼.

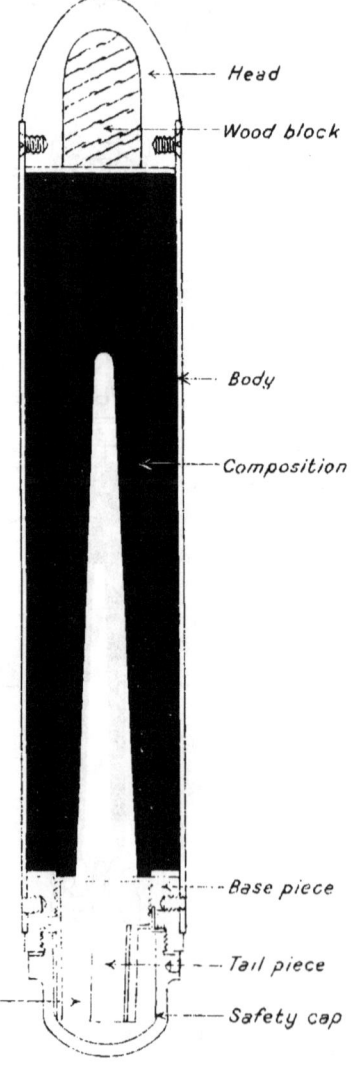

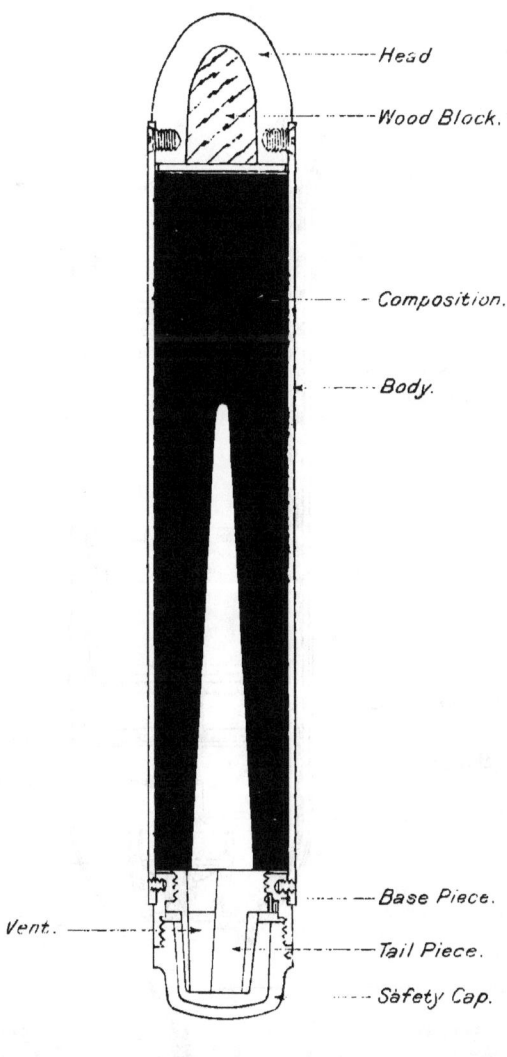

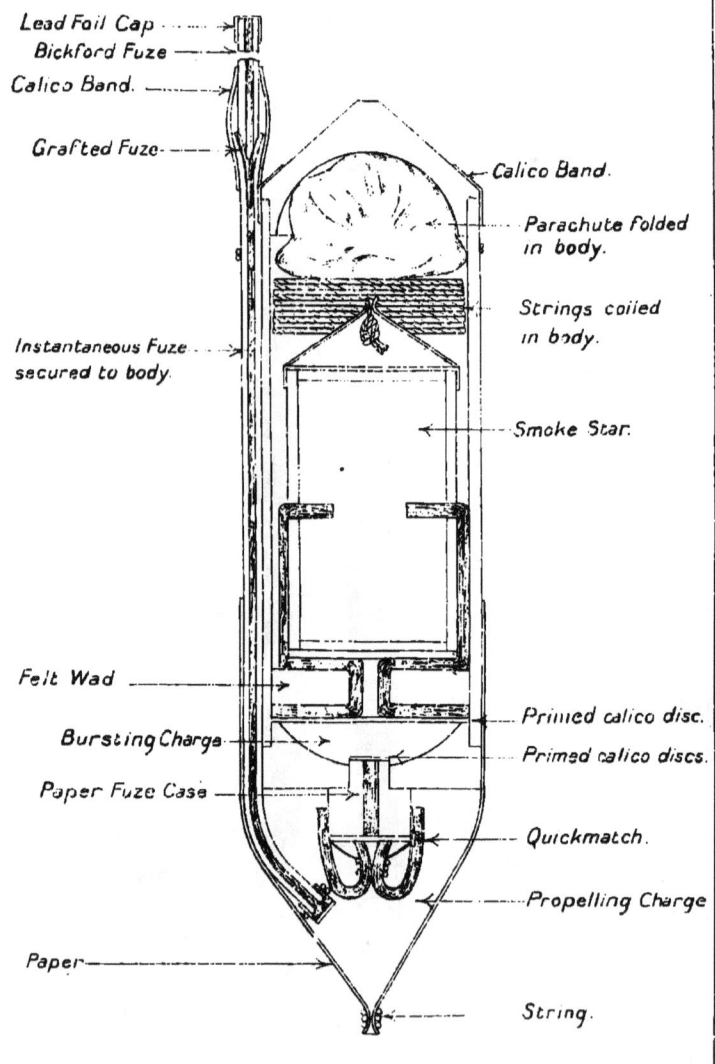

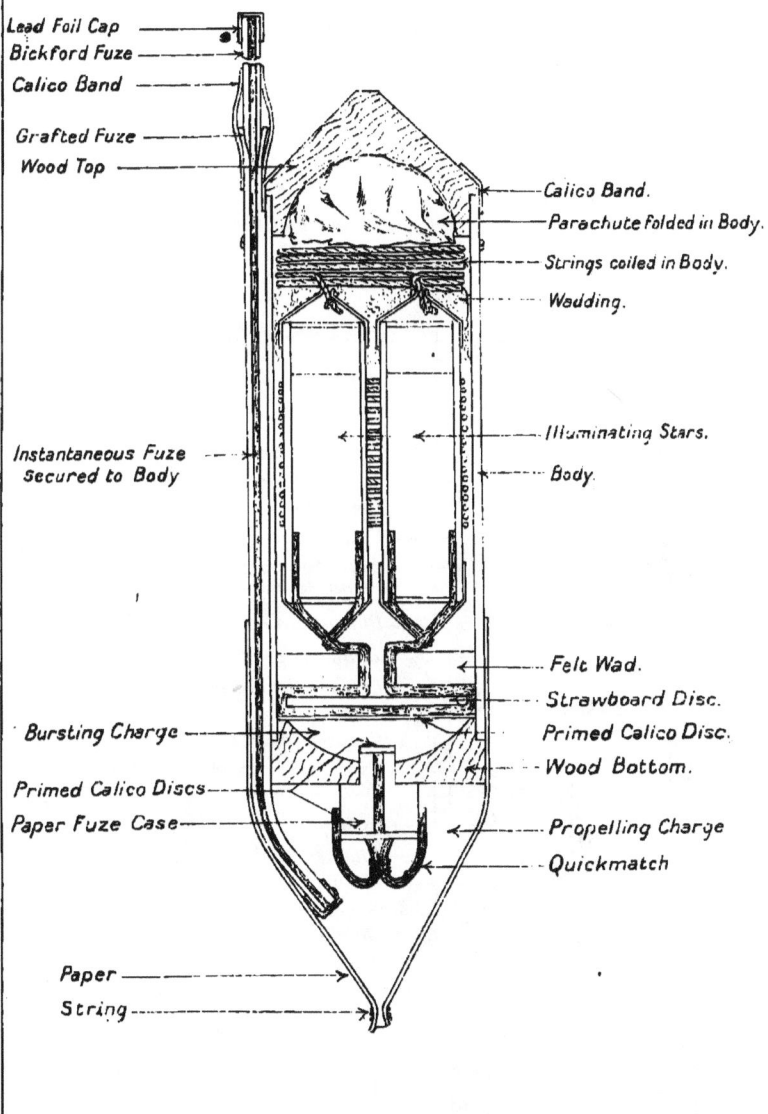

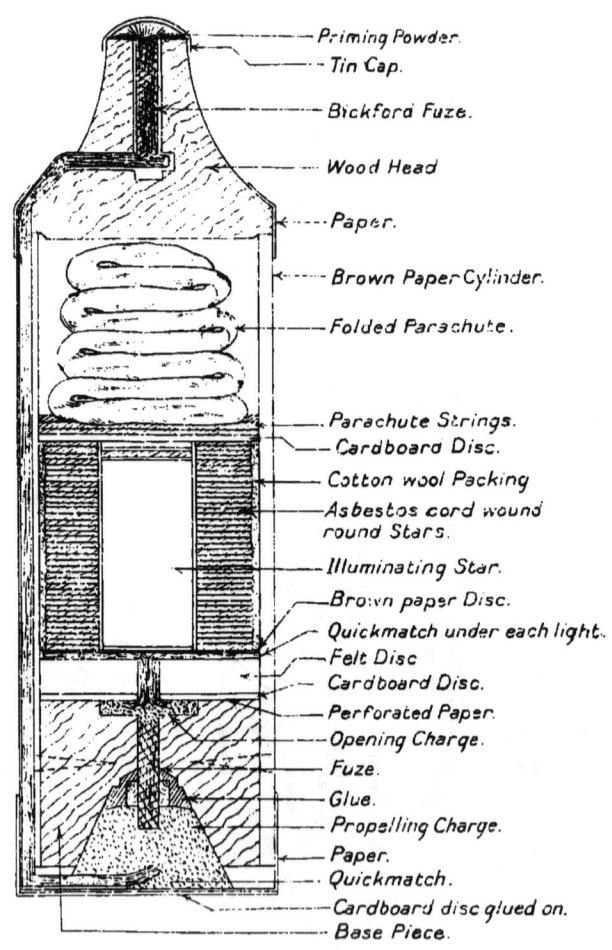

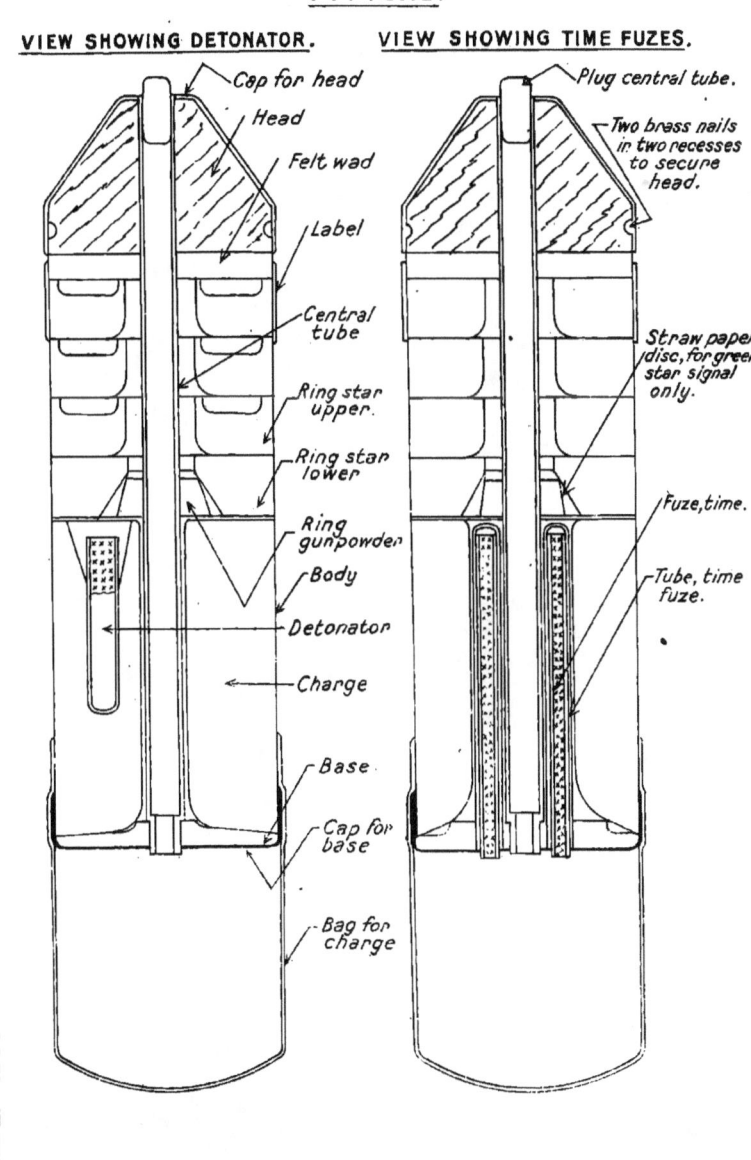

www.ingramcontent.com/pod-product-compliance
Lightning Source LLC
Chambersburg PA
CBHW070202100426
42743CB00013B/3022